Soli
Deo
Gloria

These Latin words mean,
To God alone be the Glory

You will also find this inscription on the last page.
We want this to be true of this book
from its beginning to its ending.

THE GOD WHO WHISPERS

PAM FERNANDO
FRAN ROSEBERRY

RML BOOKS
PROSPER, TEXAS

THE GOD WHO WHISPERS
Copyright © 2021 Pam Fernando and Fran Roseberry

ISBN Paperback 978-1-7343079-7-9
ISBN eBook 978-1-7358461-1-8

Book Cover design by Blu Design Concepts, Nashville, TN
Cover Photograph by Clive Fernando, Plano, Texas

Published by RML Books
1080 Firewheel Lane
Prosper, Texas 75078

www.RMLBooks.com

Printed in the United States of America

TABLE OF CONTENTS

Foreword 7

Acknowledgements 13

Introduction..15

1. It Started Here...............................21

2. I Want You to Know....................27

3. I Made This Just for You............35

4. He's Got it Covered 41

5. Use Your Imagination.................47

6. Let Go and Let God Handle It 53

7. God Transforms............................59

8. Obedience is Better than Sacrifice 65

9. I Will Save You.............................71

10. All for the Glory of God 77

11. It's Not About Me, It's About Him..............85

12. I Am Listening.............................89

13. Be My Hands and Feet 95

14. Help My Unbelief.........................101

15. Burden of Unforgiveness............109

16. I Have Plans for You 117

17. Living for the Glory of God.....................123

Some Final Thoughts (Pam & Fran) 131

ℱOREWORD

Slow down! Be still! Listen! Those words are like warnings when said forcefully. However, we remember that God has spoken to prophets and kings in prayerful, hushed tones, so why not to two women who trusted and obeyed the urges—that inner voice—calling them to do the improbable?

Pam Fernando, from Sri Lanka and Fran Roseberry of New York, are two women who might never have met but were brought together in Texas through their church. I know these women and they are zealous for The Lord. They love Him and their zeal seems to draw them into a sacred nearness with God that allows them to experience incredible insights and peace. Their friendship, forged in prayer, has led them to do something a bit far-fetched—to coauthor a book—to share the narrations of their intimate stories of spiritual awakenings. Their good will has brought us this powerful book—with miracles, gentle healings, missionary service to the poor and needy and restoration of broken relationships.

It is so good to know that our all-powerful God still whispers in this day to those who will trust and obey His call.

I am privileged, and deeply moved to lend my voice to this incredible endeavor, for these stories have convicted me to be more trusting and obedient to God's whisperings in my own life.

Be still. Listen.

—Patty Woodmansee
CHRISTIAN TEACHER, SPEAKER, AND WRITER

For the glory of God, for walking with us,
and caring for us in this life journey together.

To our husbands, Clive, and David, for their gracious
support and love throughout our journey together.

ACKNOWLEDGEMENTS

My great appreciation for our editor Bruce Barbour and his wife Karen Ann Moore, for their constant and endearing encouragement and prayers throughout the writing of this book.

Also, our prayer partners who prayed for God's guidance in writing this book. Especially to Karen Bedford, who gave selflessly while working with me, stretching, and guiding me throughout this process. I am deeply grateful for her thoughts, tenderness, and toughness. Without her I could not have done my part in this book the way God wanted it to be.

And for you, Fran, my soul sister, I wouldn't have attempted this, and couldn't have accomplished this, without you! To God be the Glory!!!

—Pam

My husband and our family have cheered me on the entire time. What a blessing it was to feel your love and support at every turn. Thank you all!

Madison Miller and Amber Gallaway, you each were there exactly at the time when I needed your expertise and encouragement. For your willing hearts and sweet spirits, I am so thankful.

Special gratitude to our editor Bruce Barbour and his gifted wife Karen Moore. You prayed for us. You prayed for this book. You have listened for God's whispers in this time as much as Pam and I have. Your contribution to this book, only God can measure. It has been a JOY to work with you.

For our Prayer Partners, thank you and God bless you.

And for you Pam, my soul sister, I wouldn't have attempted this, and couldn't have accomplished this, without you! To God be the Glory!!

—Fran

INTRODUCTION

Pam

The idea of this book is borne out of an unlikely friendship, but one that grew out of a love for God and His many ways of delighting and surprising us with His glory and presence. Fran and I first came together through our shared church and a desire for prayer. From there, our friendship grew and was forged in our mutual awe of what a personal God we love.

One day when telling Fran how I found a silver necklace with a cross on the sidewalk and how God spoke to me through that moment, Fran interrupted me, saying we should write these stories down and share them. To my surprise, I instantly agreed, as I did again when Fran said that we should call our stories, 'The God Who Whispers'! We soon recognized that throughout the entire conversation, the Holy Spirit was at work within us both, because we knew we would not dare to think of this on our own. We had no idea what we were getting ourselves into!

As soon as we both hung up, God started to speak to us, separately. Fran soon texted me saying that we should write a book. I replied saying, "Yes, let's pray." That night I was petrified, understanding it was an impossible task for me. So, I prayed, "Lord, if this is Your Will, I am willing, but let me know it is really from You." I asked God within one month's period that someone would speak to Fran and volunteer to be our writer. I never told Fran I had asked for this confirmation from God. When I mentioned it to my friend Karen, she asked, "What if Fran will not tell?" I replied, "She will," because I knew if it's God's will, He has to make it known to me.

It didn't take a month, but within two days Fran texted me, "Pam, you won't believe this! When I sought prayer from my prayer group, one of the young members, Madison Miller, said she would like to help us write our book!" This indeed was my God confirming for me, as I had asked this of Him! From there on out, I never looked back. Soon, Madison had to move away, but even before she moved out, God whispered to me that my friend Karen Bedford is a writer, and she has the skills you will need to help you write your stories. Once again, my loving Father provided for me, for when I presented what God had told me to Karen, she submitted, despite her own doubts, as she had come to trust fully in God's whispers to me.

When you enjoy the presence of God through His daily whispers and the sweetness of His love, things of earth will grow strangely dim in the light of glory and grace. The delight and joy of the Lord surpasses the pain and suffering of the work you are called to do for His glory.

It is the Creator's desire to communicate Himself to His created. We only need to seek God daily in simple moments and entertain His presence, for Him to start to communicate and reveal His glory. However, this does not come overnight. Discerning God's whispers takes practice. Think of it as training to improve a skill. Then without thought, you'll be turning to Him frequently to enjoy these mysterious whispers and then suddenly, you'll find your prayer life has become more active and alive! This will become easier and even be more natural than breathing when you have been trained by whispers.

From my earliest memory, nothing pleased me more than to seek Jesus in my daily life. As far back as I can remember, prayer has always been the most important part of it all. But it wasn't until later as an adult, that I came to know and recognize His whispers.

My first memory of hearing the voice of God was 17 years ago when I heard my name being called. Oddly, it was my middle name, which hardly anyone uses now, except my husband and family. It was when I was grocery shopping, I heard "Anoma" coming from a different aisle in the store. Instinctively, I assumed that my husband was calling for me and I went to look for him. I chuckled as it dawned on me that I came alone and I thought to myself, "I've been married so long that I hear him when he's not even with me."

A few months later, while I was shopping, the exact same thing happened again! Once back home, I recalled the scripture passage from 1 Samuel 3:19 where the Lord called Samuel, but he wasn't sure who it was who was calling him. When Samuel told his teacher Eli, he instructed Samuel to reply by saying 'Speak, Lord, for your servant is listening.' Thinking of this, I decided to reply the same way if I heard my name being called again.

Not long after, while in a department store, I heard loud and clear "Anoma." Without thinking, I turned around and replied, "Yes?" fully expecting to see my husband. Again, my husband was not with me! Remembering Samuel, I closed my eyes on the spot and whispered, "Yes my Lord, your servant is listening." I heard nothing back, nor perceived any significance in hearing my name being called, so I soon forgot it.

But now, in hindsight, I trust it was the beginning of God getting my attention by way of His Holy whispers. These audible whispers allowed me to start to recognize the many other ways God uses to communicate with us... the many ways He 'whispers' to us in our daily moments. His Holy whispers always benefit someone. Whether it benefits me for my own joy and peace or if it's meant for someone else's, it is ALWAYS done for the glory of God.

Creator God can use anything of His creation to speak to His created:

- It could be a person who accidentally speaks the answer to what you are looking for.

- It could be through scripture or while meditating on it.

- It could be just to be still and enjoy His presence.

- It could be communicated through singing, praising and worship.

- It could be a strong compulsion within you that does not go away.

- It could be through dreams and visions.

- It could be a voice within you for your enjoyment or for the sake of others.

- It could be nature that demonstrates and reflects the glory of God.

- It could be through pain and suffering.

- It could be a heart shaped rock, a cross-shaped leaf or a cloud resembling an angel...

- It could be even unwanted grass clippings which represent a cross, or a dirty unrecognizable penny which directs you to prayer.

One of my sister's-in-law believes that when God wants to confirm something for her, she will find feathers in the most unlikely places. After listening to her stories, now, I too believe that God is whispering to her through feathers, so I will pray for her when I come across a feather, as I know it to be God's reminder to me to cover her concerns in prayer, and it has been proven out over time that it is His prompting to pray for her. Isn't it amazing how God puts us together in prayer through His whispers?

It's my hope after reading our personal and yet true stories that you will be opened to allow God to draw you closer to Him through these gentle whispers. He uses them to guide and connect us with Him and with others, just like Fran connected with me. We all have different callings, and God shows us the path to fulfilling our own. He wants us to participate through and with Him in this world for all of our benefits. How humbling it is that our Creator wants to be in our lives, in an interactive, real-time relationship with us! God doesn't need us, He wants us, and He is right here, right now. Ask Him to help you release your doubts and enable you to become aware of His ways. He will not let you down, in fact, He will delight in you and you will be overcome with joy!!

Let Him guide you through this book. Expect to see and hear Him!!!

Fran

This book may reveal a God you have not imagined possible. If, after you read the stories we share in this book you find yourself thinking that the events were purely coincidental, please don't give up, but instead read on. These stories are true. They happened to us. Often, we experienced them with other people, but sometimes it was simply God speaking to us, as in a whisper.

As Pam and I shared these experiences with each other, we began to recognize that God wanted to be involved, and actually was involved, in our day to day lives. Those times brought to life a relationship with God that was intimate, real, exciting, helpful, and full of love. If He wants that kind of relationship with us, we believe He wants that kind of relationship with you.

Pam and I are expecting that many of you, as you read, will resonate with what we are sharing. You will recall times when you heard God speak also...like in a whisper. We think that by putting the word "whisper" to the voice that we have experienced, you will be prompted by a memory or experience similar to one of ours. We have provided blank pages in the back of this book for you to record your thoughts. Jot down your whispers on one of those pages and plan on going back later to remember and process what happened.

We want to caution you that there are other forces that speak into our lives that are not of God. These forces also sound like whispers. Forces like our culture, our own broken nature, and also the devil, can communicate with our minds. We must be extremely careful to recognize the source. It is critical to remember that God would never say anything that is contrary to what He has already said in His Word, in the Bible. We must always be able to confirm a directive solidly in the words of Scripture. If you can do that, you will know it is the Lord speaking to you... and you will feel His peace!

To state this clearly, what Pam and I want to show you is that the God of the Bible, when He chooses, actually does whisper to us, and far more frequently than most of us imagine!

1

ᏆT STARTED ᎻERE

Jesus looked at them and said,
"With man this is impossible,
but with God all things are possible."
MATTHEW 19:26

"Our Towel Story" (Pam and Fran)
In the past few years, we have had many sweet times of prayer that bonded us together in a very deep kinship. In our times together, we experience God in much the same way. He whispers to both of us. Many times. We are women from different backgrounds, cultures, families of origin and upbringing, but in the Lord, we are kindred spirits. It is as if we have the same heart. We overflow with joy as we embrace this unity in His Spirit. There's no fear of judgment in our friendship...only love.

But in March of 2019, our love of God brought each of us into a special awareness of His love and interest in our lives! The story of what happened to both of us prompted us to write this book, and the story began with a whisper.

We both have a special love for yellow flowers. We

both know that Fran especially loves yellow sunflowers. So, when she moved into her new apartment, I (Pam) was hoping to bless her and give her a set of dish towels with yellow sunflowers on them. It would be the perfect gift.

One day, I set out to find the perfect set of towels in the mall. While shopping in one store, I couldn't help but notice a set of towels with the scripture, 'With God all things are possible.' They were nice enough, but they didn't have any sunflowers on them. I saw them on the store shelf, and I was about to pass by when I heard a small voice in my head saying, "That's for Fran." But I was looking for towels that had sunflowers, Fran's favorite yellow flower, not a Bible verse. I argued with this voice, insisting, "No, I want yellow sunflower towels for her!" I continued to search without any success in finding what I wanted to give her.

As I was about to leave the store empty handed, I saw the scripture towels again. And I heard again, "That's for Fran. Fran will love this verse." And then I heard this: "By the way, there is a set of two; one for you and one for her."

Suddenly, I realized that these whispers were not my random thoughts; it wasn't my voice I had heard. They were whispers or promptings from God. Instantly, I relinquished my plan for yellow towels and surrendered to God's leading. I bought the scripture towels.

The next time we were together, Pam gave me (Fran) the towels. Upon opening the package, I heard a whisper, "Give one to Pam; they both have the same verse," so I said, "Pam, one towel is for you and one is for me!" And without hesitation Pam thanked me and accepted the towel. (After all, this is what she had heard in the store!)

Normally, it is awkward to take back part of a gift one gives, but we have a special relationship; a friendship that is grounded in our shared love of God. Pam shared with me what God had whispered in the store and both of us were able to rejoice in what God had done. But there was much more to come.

Later that day, we sat down for lunch and shared stories about God moving in our lives and the people we know. But as we got up from lunch, I (Fran) accidentally knocked a water glass on the floor. We looked at each other and said, "Our towels!" and without pausing a second, we each ran to grab our towels and seconds later, on our knees, we were wiping up the spill.

After it had been wiped dry, we each began to realize what was happening. God was gently whispering to each of us. He was saying to us, "Look what I have provided for each of you. I knew this would happen. Nothing in your lives is insignificant to me. Through me...all things are possible."

This was, of course, the exact Scripture passage on our newly wet towels.

We looked at each other, and delighted and humbled we said, "Who else could have planned this! Only God!"

We both had the next idea at the same time. "Camera!" we said and reached for our mobile phones to document this moment.

Later, after having so much fun over this silly spill, Pam said, "Fran, you did not even apologize for spilling the water!" She answered, "How could I say I was sorry for something so wonderful and fun?"

Our God gives us many opportunities to laugh and have fun, even in small and silly ways like this. We think that our Lord takes delight in all our giggles and laughter, and we both felt it. He is a God who is with us in the good and bad, as well as the silly and the challenging times. He is there for us in times of joy and especially, in times of pain and suffering.

Fran's towel was no longer just a dish towel. It became a holy towel, which she would never wash again. Pam also has not washed her towel since that afternoon. Each of us has kept the towel, just as they were that day, in special places of devotion and prayer in our own homes. Each of these towels serve now as a reminder of a series of simple events that revealed God's love and presence. All of this happened because He whispered.

Often, we miss God's grander plans for us because we are attached to our own thoughts and plans. Usually, our pride prevents us from surrendering because we trust more in our thoughts and plans, thinking that they are best, and inadvertently, placing these plans before God's plan for us!

God is willing and ready, even before we call for help. Since then, with all our visits and meals together, there has never been another accidental spill. This was the only time we had spilled water and what we had needed to clean it up had already been provided through the God who whispers.

But there is more….

The Lord continued to use this event. A few days later, while I (Pam) was preparing a presentation for some supporters of my mission trip to India, God whispered again, "Share the towel story with your supporters." This time I excitedly agreed with Him. I told Him that I would call Fran the next morning and let her know that God wants these supporters to hear the simple and silly story about our towels. I realized that these stories are created through His whispers. They are important. God whispered back to me saying, "Wait until she comes for the presentation and when you ask her to tell the story about the towels, she will tell you, "I will do whatever you say, Pam."

In the Bible, there is a story about a godly man named Elijah. God told Elijah to go out and stand on a mountain to see God's presence pass by. Though Elijah saw many powerful miracles of God, He met God through the gentle whisper. As I understood this, its simplicity and small daily moments created an intimacy with Him allowing us to appreciate the miracles in a deeper way.

> *The LORD said, "Go out and stand on the mountain in the presence of the LORD, for the LORD is about the pass by." Then a great and powerful wind tore the mountains apart and shattered the rocks before the LORD, but the LORD was not in the wind. After the wind there was an earthquake, but the LORD was not in the earthquake. After the earthquake came a fire, but the LORD was not in the fire. And after the fire came a gentle whisper. When Elijah heard it, he pulled his cloak over his face and went out and stood at the mouth of the cave.*
>
> 1 KINGS 19:11-13

That night I met Fran at the door, and asked her, "Would you be willing to share the story about the towels before I give my presentation?" And just as God had assured, Fran answered, "Pam, I will do whatever you tell me." Fran does not like to be in the spotlight, so I was surprised at how quickly she had agreed. To encourage her, I told her that God had whispered her response to me on the previous night.

We believe that it is important to God for us to share our daily walk and the stories of how He communicates with us; how He whispers to us. So, even though I am not comfortable speaking in front of groups of people, I (Fran) told the towel story just as it had happened. People had come that night to hear stories about ministry and miracles from Pam's mission trip to India, and they did. But that night, our towel story was a simple moment of noticing His presence in our daily lives. After the presentation, many people came up to let us know that the towel story was their favorite part of the evening!

We have thought that the Towel Story was just our story to tell. But we have come to understand that it isn't our story only. It's God's story and we are telling it for Him. As you have seen, He was directing the story with His whispers. We try to be obedient participants. When we hear a whisper from God, a directive, we obey Him (even if Pam had to argue a little). If Pam had said no to buying those matching towels, and if I hadn't shared them and given one back to her, and if we hadn't used the towels to clean up the spill of water, we would not have recognized how God Himself knew all that was to happen. We would not have realized that He had even provided the means for both of us to clean up the spill together. It also meant that we had a story to share with Pam's missionary supporters, a story that excited the entire group.

"And once we start hearing the gentle whispers,
we will then be ready for miracles."
RICHARD FOSTER

We have told this story of the towel many times since. This book, "The God Who Whispers," is the most recent telling of God's stories. We hope you are encouraged to: Listen for God's whispers. Obey them. And as you do, He will bless you.

2

I Want *Y*ou to *K*now

Delight yourself in the Lord
and He will give you the desires of your heart.
Psalm 37:4

"Pray for My Heart and My Will" (Pam)

Why do we pray if we do not know what happens when we pray? On the other hand, if God knows our needs, even before we ask for them, why do we have to pray? Isn't it just a waste of time? I have wondered about many of these things and I have even dared to ask the Lord! I hope this story will change the way you pray, allowing you to trust more fully in God.

I was praying day and night for someone who was experiencing a difficult situation for nearly five years. During this period, every time I woke up in the night, I would go to my knees to cover this person in prayer. I love to kneel when I pray, because it is very humbling for me when I am talking to my Creator, the God of this Universe.

One night as I was awakened to pray for this person, God whispered to me, "Enough of your loved ones, now pray for My Heart and My Will and I will take care of yours." Actually, it was more like someone shouting than a whisper; it was a command! No one other than my sleeping husband was in the room. I knew it was from the Lord, but it was difficult to obey because I was going through one of the lowest times of my life. Throughout this, prayer was the only thing that sustained me, giving me the living hope, and the strength I needed to walk upright and keep going. Now my Lord has asked me to stop praying for my own needs.

I was unable to understand then, but as I have grown and become more mature in my prayer life, I know that Jesus is ENOUGH in every circumstance. He paid the price for all of us whether we acknowledge it or not. He only wanted to redeem me from my fears, doubts and uncertainties about life and give me joy, even in the most difficult times. I had a choice to make: Am I going to pray for His Heart and His Will or for my heart and my will?

At this moment, I realized that I had taken too much comfort in prayer for my own gain. What I didn't see was that I had failed to delight in the Lord and trust Him to delight in me. If I delight in Him, His Heart and His Will become more important to me, and when He delights in my obedience, we become completely aligned, and all my desires are therefore His and they will be met.

If you love and care for someone, won't you care for their daily needs before being asked? I reluctantly, and slowly started my journey to pray for God's Heart and God's Will. In my times of struggle, my Lord would guide me with a name or give me visions of people in distress and I took delight in praying for them even though they were strangers to me. During my set prayer times, I would still pray for my loved ones as well as for prayer requests from all over the world. But now all other prayer times were devoted to praying for God's Heart and His Will for His children. That completely removed my fears from the things I am called to do during the day.

As I started to delight in this kind of prayer and trust my Lord for all my needs, all the names and visions stopped. Then doubt crept in, especially on the days when I was tired and extremely sleepy, as I was being woken up several times from sleep to get on my knees and pray. This is the day I realized how cleverly we can use scripture for our own gain. My mind started to act out. I told myself, God is the same yesterday, today and forever (Hebrews 13:8), and He can do everything without me involved. What gain do I have by going on my knees in the wee hours? Perhaps I am acting like God by praying for His Will over His children. So, on my knees I whispered, questioning God, "You are my Lord and my God; you can do anything in a flash without my prayer. Am I wasting my time on my knees thinking you want me to pray for Your Heart and Your Will for Your children?" I never heard a reply, so I prayed, willing to be His fool, thinking my Lord wanted me to pray for His Heart and His Will for His children.

The next day was Tuesday, a day I usually enjoy going to church. One of our priests met me at the door saying they wished to speak with me after church. As we met together, this priest stretched out his arms with pure joy and said, "Look at me, look at me, I am healed." Seeing my confused face, the priest said "I have been sick for a while and I have seen many doctors. But you came to me last night in my dreams and prayed over me and I woke up immediately healed." Tears welled up in my eyes because I never knew this priest was sick and I felt sad that I had never prayed for him.

That night, on my knees before my Lord, I began to give thanks and praise for what He had done for this priest, despite me never praying for him specifically. Immediately, God replayed my question from the night before, "Am I wasting my time on my knees, thinking you want me to pray for Your Heart and Your Will for Your children?" Then He whispered, "This is your answer." From that day forward, I never doubted praying for His Heart and His Will for His children. It became joyful for me to delight in His calling while allowing Him to delight in my obedience to His calling. It became a very humbling and joyful thing to pray for the Glory of God without expecting any returns and without wanting to know how He was going to use my prayers. When your desire becomes His desire, all your desires are met by His desires. They all become one!

Be careful not to twist the scripture for your own sinful gain. Always go to God in prayer and ask questions of Him for clarification. Have you ever doubted the existence of God, or what He might be showing you? Never be afraid to question God. He can handle all our doubts and uncertainties, just because of who HE IS. HE IS GOD!

"I Want You to Know" (Fran)

Have you ever received an opportunity that you never expected or planned for? This is exactly what happened to my husband David. It was 1993 and he was out of town at a board meeting when one of the board members approached David. He came right to the point. "God told me in a dream last night that I am to send you and your wife to Israel." David was surprised, and I'm sure polite, but didn't believe him. When David returned home and explained the man's offer, I shared his surprise! We were new in ministry and had never heard a message like this, so not knowing any better, we dismissed it and went on with life.

Six months later at the next board meeting, the man again approached David, asking him if he had made the arrangements for the trip. David confessed that he hadn't. The gentleman asked David what he needed to move ahead, and my husband honestly told him "Money." The man pulled out his checkbook and wrote him a check. We were going to Israel.

David is an Anglican priest and we thought that at some point we would have the opportunity to go to the Holy Land. As romantic as it sounds, this trip would require a huge step of faith for each of us. David would have to release control of our young burgeoning church in Plano, Texas, and I would have to leave our four young children to travel halfway around the world. Still, we knew we could no longer refuse to go for two reasons; we had the money to go, and we were afraid to question that God had arranged it! So, we enrolled in a three-week course of study and touring at a college overlooking the ancient walled city of Jerusalem.

I remember the anticipation I personally had about the trip. I had been involved in a very intensive Bible study. The study had taken us back and forth through the Old and New Testaments. I recall how exciting it was to read all the stories about characters of all kinds, humans like you and me. Some were extraordinarily faithful, all were flawed, and a few were famous for their part in revealing God and His ways. Through the scriptures I had begun to know God and it was so exciting. What I couldn't have known was that God was preparing to teach me even more about Himself and His Word on this trip...in a whisper.

The professors led us across the stunning countryside of Israel visiting one Bible site after another. We walked where Jesus walked. It was thrilling for all of us. To my surprise, and disappointment, I was struggling to remember any of the information from my Bible study. I've never been one to remember details, but I had been longing to connect my growing love for God with Scripture and the land. I was privately very frustrated. I began to complain. I was complaining to the God I had come to know. As my frustration mounted, I heard myself asking God, "What was the point of me studying the Bible?" It was then I heard His answer in a whisper. "I want you to know that My Word is alive." I hadn't expected to hear anything. I hadn't expected to hear this. His whisper changed my understanding of the Bible and deeply impacted my relationship with Him. When I heard these words, I felt such peace and joy! Today, everything about my relationship with God has changed!

Consider this: God HAD A PLAN!

- He chose a man named Herb who knew Him.

- He knew Herb would obey Him.

- He spoke to Herb in a dream.

- God had provided the means for our trip through His blessing of Herb.

- God knew that David and I would go to Israel.

- And He knew things about me.

- He knew I had been in a Bible Study and was falling in love with Him.

- He knew I was beginning to understand Him and His ways.

- He heard and understood my question, "Why can't I remember?"

- He had planned His answer.

- He knew I would hear Him whispering...even for the first time.

- He knew His answer was much more important than the question I was asking.

- He knows that He changed my life that day...through a whisper.

- He was telling me not only that His Word is alive, but He is alive and real!

The Bible is not just a collection of stories and poetry. It is not only about history and crazy characters of the past, nor is it about a fictional, lifeless God, and a pretend religion. The stories are true, and the people lived. There is an active part that Scripture has in our daily lives whether we realize it or not. God proved to me that He speaks to people today. He wants to be a part of our lives. He speaks in dreams, through His people, in His Word, and even in whispers.

Here is something else God knew when He spoke to Herb that night in the dream. God knew it wouldn't be David's and my last trip to Israel. Through our experiences of God and His Word and exploring His Promised Land during that trip in 1994, David and I would grow to love Him more. God knew that out of that love would blossom a travel ministry that would span almost thirty years and over thirty trips. David and I have led over a thousand pilgrims to The Holy Land, to walk where Jesus walked, to connect the Scriptures we read at home with the land and lives of people who live in Israel today. God is real and He is alive. And He really does speak today...and sometimes He speaks in whispers!

3

𝓘 Made 𝓣his 𝓙ust for You

The heavens declare the glory of God;
the skies proclaim the work of his hands.
Psalm 19:1

"I Made this Cross Just for You" (Pam)

God often uses the sky to reveal His glory. I can't tell you how many times I have looked at the sky in awe! In these moments, His presence becomes so real, it is as though I can really feel Him standing next to me, enjoying my pure delight of His creation.

A while back, on a July 4th, around 8 PM, I received a call for prayer. Someone's husband could not breathe. Initially my response was an immediate concern for his health, and I asked if they had health insurance, and why they were not headed to the ER? She persisted with her request for me to pray for her husband. Although I felt it was more sensible for them to go directly to the hospital, how could I refuse a simple plea for prayer?

As I was speaking with her, I happened to look out my kitchen window, and I saw the most vibrant and bloody cross in the sky. This cross was made by the sunlight filtering through the branches and leaves of the oak tree in my backyard. At the core of the cross was an epicenter of bright red blood with rays emanating up, down, and across, creating a perfect Cross. Could it be a coincidence? Of course not. It was His whisper to me, a divine confirmation from God to encourage me to do the impossible. A great joy rushed over me, encouraging me to pray over the sick man. God's whispers always encourage me to obey excitedly. It helped me to overcome my human inclination and to trust the all-powerful God.

The next morning the man's wife called again to say that they never needed to go to the ER because he started to breathe soon after I prayed over the phone. She thanked me and wanted me to know that her husband was well and that he had already returned to work that morning! They made a humble plea for prayer; I chose to obey God's confirmation of their request and the prayer was fulfilled through and for God's Glory!!

That next evening, I took my usual seat at the kitchen table looking out the window, wanting to investigate that beautiful cross. It was nowhere to be seen. I even ventured out to inspect the tree and see if I could imagine how the cross could have been created by the sun streaming through its branches. The cross was the glory of God, proclaiming the work of His Hands. It was yet another heavenly mystery I would not understand.

Have you ever had any simple requests? How have you responded to these opportunities that challenge your common sense? My hope is that in hearing stories like this one, you will seek God's whispers so you too can grow in deep faith for the glory of God!

"I Love Variety" (Fran)

One day this past spring, I was admiring a peony blossom that was on my daughter's kitchen table. She loves flowers, maybe as much as I do, and she had pointed out the arrangement in the center of her table.

The blossom was amazing. Endless shades of gentle pinks folded one petal into the next. Way too many petals to count or imagine. No rhyme or reason to the gathering of them, just gracefully connected somewhere below sight, deep within the blossom. What a sweet moment to consider the beauty of God's creation. Lovely. "Thank you Lord, for surrounding us with such beauty, and for reminding me that it is everywhere if we remember to look." I continued with my visit and eventually was on my way home.

Just one more stop before I get home, the grocery store. As I entered the store, an intense spot of yellow distracted me from my list and mission. Sunflowers mixed in the various arrangements of flowers, smartly located at the front of the grocery store had caught my attention. Flowers strategically placed there to tempt most women and remind smart men. Flowers. They really can change our world. A gift of surprise, an offering for healing, a touch of love. They can say: "I'm sorry," "I love you!" "Congratulations," "Thinking of you," or all kinds of things. Flowers are a gift!

That day for me, looking more carefully at that sunflower blossom in my hand, I heard a whisper from God. "I AM a creative God, and I love variety." I looked with amazement at the intricate, perfect, structure of the center of the sunflower. It was the most perfect geometric pattern I had ever seen. It was absolutely magnificent. I studied it more closely. With amazing precision, the gorgeous gold petals, radiated out from the large, hard, dark brown, center core. "This is so impressive, God!" I whispered back to Him.

And then I remembered the pink peony. What amazing contrasts Lord! Here was a beautiful, highly structured, stiff, and strong sunflower in my hand. It was a prize. And then I remembered the sweet, lovely, tender, abundant beauty of the peony blossom. "Lord, you are amazing. Such diversity. Such creativity! Thank you for showing me how much You clearly love and value the variety in Your Creation."

I began to think about His words and what He was really telling me beyond the beauty of nature and flowers. I began to think about people, His favorite part of creation! Look back at my story for a minute. Compare the difference in the wild blossom of a peony and the intricate structure of a sunflower blossom. They are as different as they can be. Can you say that one is better than the other? One is more perfect than the other? One more loved by God than the other? Absolutely not!

If creation is evidence of the joy God has in creating, and if we believe He has created each of us to be unique, shouldn't we also look at every person, every group, every race, every difference, as part of God's mysterious and wonderful design and creativity? Everything we see is an expression of His plan, and a part of His heart! Since He loves each and every part...wouldn't we? Shouldn't we?

"I Made this Leaf Just for You" (Fran)

God's creation can teach us even more if we take the time to look.

When you can, find a quiet spot where you can observe nature. Perhaps you can sit outside, or look through a car window, take a walk, or even just look up at the sky...what do you see?

Take a moment to focus in on the branch of a tree, or a particular flower, maybe a blade of grass or something else from nature. Now look more carefully. Look more intentionally. Pick one thing to study. Pick one leaf, or one blossom. You might be looking at a whole row of identical birds on a telephone wire and then pick one special bird. Perhaps a cloud formation will catch your imagination. Take a minute to study it: shape, color variations, details.

Now hear these words that God could be whispering to you. "I made this leaf just for you!" or "That bird up on that wire, third from the right, yes, that one, I made him for you!"

Think about it seriously! Do you think that anyone else in the world will ever see that leaf, or bird, or cloud? Isn't it possible that God made that leaf with you in mind? Isn't that a remarkable thought? It's about the intimacy of an amazing God. In the abundance of His creation and love, He could have been thinking of me or you as He was working.

It is a mysterious idea for adults. It is a magical idea to share with children. To a child it can help explain how important they are and how special they are to God. It speaks to God's incredible magnitude...His awareness and love for each of us. How wonderful it is to capture a child's imagination and connect them to our most creative and personal God. Take the time to look and listen. Hear God whispering, whether for a child or to an adult, "I made this just for you!" and consider all He means!

4

*H*E'S GOT IT COVERED

Children are a heritage from the Lord,
offspring a reward from him.
PSALM 127:3

"OK, Lord" (Pam)

Our children and grandchildren are a treasured gift from God for a designated period of time. Therefore, we must take every opportunity to set a good example in how we live out our faith.

One of the blessings I have enjoyed as a grandmother is taking my only granddaughter, Bethel along on my Honduras mission trips. We have been doing medical missions together in Honduras since 2017.

On one trip, we were waiting for the medical staff to arrive so we could begin our work. There was quite a bit of chaos in the halls as concerned employees were trying to open the Optical clinic and the door could not be opened. Apparently, six different people had tried to open the door, but the key would not go in. When I saw the chaos, I started to giggle, and Bethel quickly asked me why I was laughing? Quietly, I leaned over and told her that they just needed to pray over it. Then she challenged me to do just that. I never push myself without being asked, but when your grandchild asks you, you don't think twice because you are supposed to set an example for them. So I got up, walked across the hall as the crowd stepped aside and I prayed over the lock. I then asked for the key, and easily opened the door to the clinic. Everyone was in awe!

Once we were back home, when Bethel's Mom was out, I heard her sharing stories with two of her brothers, Enoch, and Gilead. I decided to join them too. They were stories of the miracles she had seen in Honduras while on mission with me. Just as she finished telling them about the broken lock and how it opened after praying over it, we all could hear someone coming up the stairs.

Hurriedly, we turned off the light and became quiet, so as not to get into trouble from their mom for being up past bedtime. One of the boys grabbed a flashlight, but it was broken. Excitedly, and in the darkness, he handed it over to me and asked quietly for me to pray over it! As they placed it in my hand, I could feel how truly broken it really was and I whispered to them that you can't get a broken flashlight to work. I didn't want to pray over it and break the faith and trust of my innocent grandchildren. But then I heard a whisper, "Pray over it, so these children will know that I am God." Trusting in His assurance, I said, "OK, Lord."

I prayed, just as God had whispered, but nothing happened. Just then, we heard footsteps going back down the stairs. Then Bethel said, "I have another flashlight," and she ran to her room, taking the broken flashlight with her. Soon after, Bethel snuck back to our room with the broken flashlight, and we could see that it was now working! Amazed by this, the boys excitedly asked, "Bethel, how did you get it to work?" She promised them that she had done nothing but lay it on the floor while she was looking for hers, and then like magic, the broken one began to work! It overwhelms me how God allows my grandchildren to see that He is the God of every moment!

I hope I am setting an example of going to God in prayer in all circumstances and that getting to know Him can be great fun. If God is with them in the little things and silly times, then they can learn to trust He will also be with them in the bigger and harder times. Are you willing to make a difference in your child and grandchild's life? You may not fix flashlights, but God will show you what He wants to do for you and yours. It's an exercise in trust. Listen, listen for His whispers, discover His leadings, and follow them, and get ready to be delighted.

God at Walmart (Fran)

I wonder if you are like me and pray to be a good example to the people around you. Even more important than being a good example, I pray that people will see my devotion to God so it will inspire them to know Him too. I especially love when my grandchildren are learning from me. Often the Lord shows me that they do notice. Sometimes I know God is at work by an amazing statement that comes out of their innocent mouths, or a perceptive prayer, or a godly gesture, and sometimes it is just a simple comment. I am immediately aware of God's presence and work in their tender lives. I am excited for them and grateful to Him.

The other day I was on my way home from my daughter's home. This was going to be a quick stop. I pulled into the Walmart parking lot and parked the car. I was about to enter the store when I heard Him whisper to me. "Look at this!"

When I hear words like this, out of the blue, I have learned it is probably God. I want to obey Him whenever I hear Him whisper.

Not knowing what to expect, still with confidence, I turned around and looked up. Up in the sky, in the center of my vision, were two distinctly straight trails made by passing jets that created a cross. This one was perfect! I stopped to admire it and said quietly, "Thank you, Lord. It's beautiful!"

Having just left my daughter's home, I thought that if my family ran outside immediately, they also would see the cross. As I was about to call them, my phone rang.

It was my grandson Moses. "Hi Mo," I said and was about to tell him to run outside with his family. I didn't have time to say anything before he was telling me about the amazing cross up in the sky that I had to see! I laughed and told him I was just calling to say the same thing. We agreed that it was wonderful and shared the moment. I was able to help him see all the connections God had made and the way He had whispered to us. Simple and easy. And then we hung up.

This appears to be a simple story but consider this... God knew there would be a cross up in the sky, a cross that I would be able to see easily in the Walmart parking lot. He knew that if He whispered to me, "Look," I would see it. He also knew at the same time, that my grandson who has learned to appreciate and notice crosses, would connect with me and call to tell me about the same cross that he could see. God not only whispered to me at Walmart, but He also whispered to my 14-year-old grandson, half a mile away. He knew He was not only connecting us to each other, but more importantly, connecting us to Him. Do you think that this is a simple story? Not to God.

Pam's and my stories are full of lessons God teaches us when He whispers. When you know what you are looking for, and know when He is the one speaking, you will then understand what He wants. I have found a way to connect with my grandchildren in the watching for crosses. These crosses aren't just a nice design, these crosses are becoming signals that remind us God is with us. What a comfort. What an encouragement. How powerful! When we remember God is with us, we are better prepared to hear His whispers and accomplish what He wants, like teaching others to know Him better.

The Pretzel and The Cross in The Closet (Fran)

I recently received a call from my youngest granddaughter Finley. She wanted to Facetime. "GiGi...look!" and she held up to her phone a little square pretzel in front of her beaming 10-year-old face. Sure enough...it had a cross in the center! I was uncertain what she wanted me to see, till she said, "See the cross?" with such excitement! She is learning to notice crosses too.

Finley, like all my children and grandchildren, is the subject of my daily prayers.

Recently, she had proudly shown me the inside of her closet. She had decorated the door with photos...beautifully arranged, from the bottom of the door to the top, and from side to side, a cross! There were pictures of friends and family, animals, and pictures of her favorite things. It is a wonderful design that she has taken a great deal of care and thought to arrange. I stood admiring it with her as she explained it and then she said, "Look!" There in the center where the arms of the cross intersect is the prayer that I had handwritten for her years before. It is the prayer I had been teaching her and had written down for her to keep. I have been saying that prayer for thirty years and God had told me to share it with her. There was the actual copy I had hand-written for Finley. I then whispered to

God, "Thank you Lord! What can I tell her now about You?" It can be a constant conversation with a loving and active God obeying His whispers when you encourage and bless others for Him.

This is the prayer that I had prayed for her that she has cherished and is learning to say herself.

"O LORD, I pray for ___ (insert names) ___,
Set us aside from ourselves, dear LORD,
and so completely fill us with Your Holy Spirit
that we become vessels through which
You can reach and touch those we are with.
Give us Your eyes to see, Your ears to hear,
Your mind to be steadfast and faithful.
Give us Your heart to love You as the one
and only God and to love what You love.
Give us Your hands to serve and Your words to speak
that in everything we say and do
we will honor and glorify You.
Amen."
PRAYER FROM KAYE KING

I want to encourage you, reader, to keep talking and teaching about God. Be listening to His whispers directing you. Take every opportunity to encourage your children's imaginations and teach them in every way you can to see Jesus, to recognize Him around them and to think about Him. No need to worry about when to say anything or what you should say. Begin to embrace the truth that He is with you, always. He is aware of all things and loves the people around you even more than you do. Listen to His whispers and then be confident and brave. Do what He says to do. Look and expect opportunities each and every day to hear and respond to His whispers.

5
USE YOUR IMAGINATION

O Lord, our Lord,
how majestic is your name in all the earth!
You have set your glory above the heavens.
PSALM 8:1

God's Favorite Color (Fran)

Many people love sunsets. Rarely do you see a beautiful sunset and say, "Oh ho hum...(yawn)...another day done, what's for dinner?" God really does seem to be showing off at the end of each day, doesn't He? Even saying, "You've had another day. You've had another gift, now, here is the bow!"

But then there are people who love sunrises! People who love sunrises are 'morning people.' They are up before the sun is rising. No coffee needed. They wake up with a song in their heads and are excited to start anything! I'm one of those people who loves sunrises!

One of the lovely things about my marriage is that both David and I love getting up early and watching the sunrise. It takes only three minutes for the sun to come up where we live. I know; I've timed it. It is always a special moment to spend those three minutes with David starting the day together. One morning we were waiting and watching. It was then that God whispered to me as David and I were admiring the first colors appearing on the horizon.

This particular sunrise had clouds, lots of interestingly shaped clouds along the horizon line. They hadn't blocked our view of the sun, but the lighting upon them was striking. David said to me, "Do you see the fish?" After a few seconds, I confessed that I didn't see it. He tried to explain where it was. I still couldn't see it and admitted it. Then I heard God whisper to me, "I love when you use your imagination." I told David what I'd heard.

All day I thought about God's whisper that morning. I wasn't thinking about my imagination, I was thinking about God's imagination. How many thousands of times had I noticed His incredible creativity and been thrilled at the vastness of His imagination!

My family is full of artists. We value creativity, originality, shapes, and colors. Our homes are full of paintings, sculpture, pottery, and beautifully woven fabrics, and we delight in all kinds of artistic things. We love using our imaginations!

I have been learning how to oil paint this past year. One of the first things I learned was a 'trick of the trade'. Before starting to paint, it is helpful to select a color you would be using throughout your painting and rub a layer of that color loosely all over the canvas. There are two reasons for this. First, it immediately brings harmony throughout your painting, and secondly, it breaks the intimidating obstacle of where and how to start to paint on a blank, very white canvas.

I was imagining God as an artist and His daily creation of sunrises and sunsets! I thought about His wonderful imagination and how He starts His creation in the sky with a sunrise every day. Then I wondered what color He chose to use as the "all over" on His canvas. The all-the-time, every day, as His backdrop color for everything! And then I knew it!

The color is blue! Of all the colors He could have chosen, and He could have chosen any color, for the whole sky, one end to the other, top to bottom, every sunrise and every sunset, every day...it's blue! And then I realized it, understood it, imagined it...God's favorite color is blue. And if you are questioning this idea...take a moment and think of the color He chose for the ocean!

God uses His imagination all the time. His creation is as varied and unique as can be! If we understand that all these differences are His choice, His joy, His plan, it seems to me that we should also enjoy the differences. Who are we to question those differences and do anything but marvel and be grateful for this world and the way He has designed it and reveals Himself every day, and I feel He begins with the sunrise!

Love Offering (Pam)

Fran and I have an ongoing disagreement over which color is God's favorite. Fran insists God's favorite color is blue, and I argue that God's favorite color must be yellow. What do you think God's favorite color is? Do you think God even has a favorite or does He love them all equally, like His children? I believe that all colors are God's favorites, or He would not have created them. And if He created them, as He did us, then all colors and people must truly delight Him!

It is not important or necessary to have a favorite color, but it is important to take a moment of enjoyment, delighting in the presence of God through them. It could be through colors, flowers, any creatures, any instance, in a feeling, or in a time shared where our spirit is captured and enraptured by simply bringing Jesus into it. When you begin to enjoy His presence, His creation will start to reveal His glory and whisper to you as you enter into a conversation with Him. This is when we come to realize how incredibly easy it is to worship God, for when we're talking with Him, we are praising Him too!

I experienced it one beautiful spring morning in Pittsburgh. I was walking to church with my son, his wife, and my grandchildren, when my granddaughter, Bethel picked a wild buttercup flower and placed it in my palm. As the sun crept through the trees and hit the tiny yellow flower, its petals started to shine and it became so vibrant, emanating a beauty like I had never contemplated. I was overwhelmed with the magnificence of the colors I was seeing! Instantly, I was in love with this tiny wildflower as it was the most precious thing I had ever seen, more precious than silver or gold.

Upon entering the church, I saw this tiny wild buttercup as even more stunning than a diamond. So, of course, I could not throw it away. I protected it, gently closing it in my hand. Then I took my seat in the church. In that moment, I was allowed to see God's profound glory and majesty reflected in the beauty of that tiny little buttercup. I whispered to God, "Lord, I have never seen such a beautiful thing in my whole life, and I want to dedicate my soul to You, so that You see my soul as beautiful as I see this tiny yellow flower." I knew I wanted and needed to live my life in a way that my soul would look like this to God. In that moment I was able to see the fullness of all of God's creation and how it reflects His glory and I wanted to live up to what I was made for by Him!!!

During the Offertory, as the collection plate was getting passed, I heard a gentle whisper, "Place it in the collection plate as a love offering for your soul." But

I struggled. What will the usher passing the plate think of me, as we are supposed to put money into the plate? I slowly opened my fingers and looked at the flower. It had started to wither, but still it was most beautiful. To anyone else, it would have no appeal at all. But at that moment in time and because of what I felt in my heart and what I could see with my eyes, it was the most precious gift I could offer. I took one last look at the flower and I placed it on the offering plate and whispered back to my God, "Lord, I offer my soul to you. May you take joy and see my soul as beautiful as you have allowed me to see this flower!" The usher looked at the withering flower and looked at me quizzically. In my humanness, I was a little embarrassed. I didn't want to draw any attention to myself, so I quietly and gently motioned for Him to move on.

From that day onward, I get deeply excited when I see yellow flowers. As I saw God's perfection through this little insignificant flower, I also started to see others as God's perfection, like flowers in His garden, beautiful and radiant. This became a continual reminder that our souls might not have any value to others, but they are more cherished and precious to God than silver or gold. With this awakening awareness, suddenly I started to see His perfection through His creation in others. Regardless of our color, gender, size or anything of this world, God sees us as His precious jewels.

Just like God's profound glory and majesty reflected in that tiny little buttercup, His glory and majesty reflect in you too. We are never beyond redemption and He desires us all to enjoy His heaven made on earth through a relationship with Him. For this reason alone, it enables me not to judge others based on what I see, and to ask God to help me to see them as He sees them.

How do you see yourself? Now that you 've heard my

story, I hope you see how God sees your soul. If there's a difference between your view of yourself and God's view, it is time to turn your life over to Him, because you are beautiful to Him. He sees you as a precious jewel. He sees you as I saw my buttercup. Wonderfully beautiful. He has you covered, and He wants you!

6

𝓛ET GO AND 𝓛ET GOD 𝓗ANDLE 𝓘T

"Ask and it will be given to you; seek and you will find;
knock and the door will be opened to you.
For everyone who asks receives;
the one who seeks finds; and to the one
who knocks, the door will be opened."
MATTHEW 7:7-8

A Valentine from Across the World (Fran)

It was the day before Valentine's Day, 1996. My son Jed was on a mission trip in the Philippines and I hadn't spoken to him in three weeks. He was traveling with a small group of youth missionaries. They were all in their late teens and although they had completed their outreach training, they were inexperienced and needed a lot of prayer. I had prayed that morning that I would be home when he called. At 1:30 AM on Valentine's Day morning the phone next to my bed rang. It had to be Jed.

"Hi Jed, how are you Hon?" I was wide awake and already thanking God that He had answered my prayer and I was home.

"Well," he said slowly, "I'm ok...now."

"What do you mean *now*?"

"I just got out of the hospital..." and he proceeded to tell me that he had developed a severe infection on his right hand. The infection had traveled up his arm and was dangerously close to his heart when he finally saw a Philippine doctor who had immediately put him in the hospital. They put him on an IV in their amputee ward! He had been there for three days and they had just released him. He felt ok. He assured me that they told him he would be fine.

I was a good mom and listened, sounded confident and encouraged him. Before we hung up, I prayed for him, assured him that he would be fine and reminded him that God loved him and was with him. As soon as we hung up, I fell apart. I knew that he had been in such danger. I remembered just how far away he was. I recognized how little control I had to help or protect my son.

In my crying and despair God whispered to me, "Come to Me in prayer."

I went to the living room couch where I would have my daily prayer time. "Thank You, Lord that You answered my prayer and had Jed call me when I was home. Thank you, God for protecting his life!" And then I asked God, "Is he still safe, Lord?"

And then I opened my eyes and looked. There sitting right in front of me was a CD of my favorite Christmas song I had neglected to put away with all the decorations. It was the recording of the song 'All Is Well', by Michael W. Smith. I stared at it and then heard God read it to me, whispering, "All is well," and immediately His supernatural peace flowed through me.

Then He whispered, "Call Keiichi." Keiichi was the

head of Jed's Prayer Team. "Lord, it's 2 AM" "Keiichi won't mind," God replied. So, I called him. Kathy, his wife, answered and I quickly explained my reason for calling. She understood and handed the phone to her husband. We spoke for a few minutes and prayed together and just before we hung up Keiichi, prompted by a whisper from God, said to me, "Fran, all is well." I slept in peace the rest of the night.

Just hours later, as I was finishing making lunches for my other three children before they left for school, the phone rang. "Hello" I answered. It was my friend Becky. She said to me, "Fran, I've never done this before, but during my prayer time this morning, God told me to call you and say, "All is well."

As I retell this story, I am reminded of the incredible series of events that took place that Valentine's Day. God proved to me that He hears my prayers. He showed me His love for Jed and His knowledge and care of him. I could trust that my son was constantly under His care and no place on this earth was too far away. God pieced together a beautiful message using a Christmas song and a network of events, love, and assurances. Powerfully, through a whisper, I learned that whether we pray for the person down the block or someone on the other side of the earth, they are within the reach of a Holy God and all is well.

"Yes, But I Wanted You to Know" (Pam)

When loving Jesus becomes more intense, that love empowers us to live a life for the will of God. Our spiritual disciplines start to become second nature to us. Prayer, going to church, loving our neighbor, to list a few, are no longer efforts in discipline, but they become a normal way of life for us, and a truly joyful life.

This love becomes so real that it is as though we can feel

His presence where we are able to live in the freedom of joy and all our fears grow strangely dim and disappear in the light of His glory and grace. However, it is nice and necessary to know our fears and weaknesses so we can respond well when God frees us and prepares us for a beautiful future. About 22 years ago, I was forced to face my biggest fears.

Many people confided in me that they had a hard time understanding how I was able to let go of our son Avin when he went to the university at the age of thirteen and lived there on his own. His academic prowess had allowed him to achieve this unusual early admission to college. I dared not say it out loud, but I was convinced that if God gave him this capability then He would also look after my son. Then one day, I received a phone call from my son's University informing me that he was unable to breathe and that he was rushed to the ER. In hearing this, fear overcame me. Suddenly I was lost and devastated thinking this could be his last day! Immediately, I phoned Nan, our Bible study group leader, to ask for prayers, and then I dropped to my knees to pray and beseech God in this terrifying moment.

As soon as I entered into prayer, my Lord started to play back the most important conversations from Avin's childhood. I started to see how much he loved God, and what a role model he had been to me, always reminding me to see Jesus in every circumstance. Over the years, he had explained to me about molecules and their interactions, and through this he taught me to believe the Bible over science whenever there might be a conflict. He was kind and helpful to all those who were in need, and never condemned anyone.

With all these childhood reminders, a sudden awareness went into me that Avin is not afraid of death, and therefore death has no sting over him. God never gives us these beautiful children to show off but maybe His purpose in Avin had been accomplished. Then a sudden thought came to me, "If today is his last day, Avin is the winner, getting to be with his God, and I am the one being left behind!" With a mixture of fear, love, hope and confidence, I started to feel God's unwavering love for Avin. So rather than petitioning before God for my son's life, I prayed, "My Lord and my God, I trust you and now I turn Avin over to you. May your will be done. If today is his last day, I will not be able to live, please help me!"

As soon as I turned over Avin to the Will of the Lord, a great PEACE welled up and consumed all of me! Instantly, I knew God would help me endure whatever His Will would be in this circumstance. Even though I was not able to be with Avin physically and hold him at his time of need, God had him covered. In this peace I also received the strength to pull myself together and call the university staff person who was with Avin. They let me know that the blockage was cleared almost immediately and that he was now breathing well. I was ecstatic and praising my God!

Greatly relieved, I was now able to see that I had just been tested. Was I willing and able to trust my God with my son's life? It was so painful to live in that moment while thinking it's your child's last day, breathing his last breath and I was not able to be there to hold him. Again, I went before my God and asked, "Lord, I have been tested. It was too painful to live that moment. You know me inside and out. Even before I went through this, you knew how I would react. Why did I have to go through such pain?"

Then I heard my Lord saying, "Yes, I know you, but I wanted you to know you."

I never realized the power of that sentence and the value of that lesson back then. Later, it became a powerful tool of instruction when helping and mentoring people in their spiritual and physical life journey. God has given us all unique gifts and talents, and by learning to know our gifts, we can apply them to overcome our weaknesses, allowing God's will to be served in our lives.

Children are a gift of God for a period of time. By releasing them to the Will of God, it releases us from our own fears and our desire to control them, which might prevent them from becoming the people God created them to be. Have you given God the glory in and through your children?

7

GOD TRANSFORMS

"Then you will know the truth,
and the truth will set you free."
JOHN 8:32

"What If Both of You Are Right?" (Pam)

Prayer is not only a matter of changing things externally, but also of working miracles in a person's inner nature. This is my story of how as I turned to my Lord in prayer over a situation, He changed my heart to see things differently. In that moment all my anger and frustration disappeared, allowing me to enjoy such peace and calmness, that I knew could only come from Him.

One day I was having an argument with my husband, whom I have been married to for nearly forty years now. We had different views on something that had happened in the past and, as it goes, both of us were convinced we were each right, and the other person was wrong. I was sure of my memory, and I felt that my husband was denying the truth purposely to win the argument.

Frustrated and unwilling to be proven wrong, I

left the conversation to go to God in prayer. I was certain that God would be on my side since I was the honest one in this situation. I got down on my knees and asked God how my husband could be lying to me.

Then, I heard a whisper from God, "What if I say you are wrong?" I knew it wasn't from me, or my thought. Would I want to condemn myself of being wrong?

This was not what I was expecting to hear. Rather than admitting to God that I could be wrong, I responded to Him saying, "That can't be. In my mind, I have a picture-perfect memory of the situation." The gentle whisper came again, and I heard God ask me, "What if I say he is right?" This was hard to hear and even harder to accept! Do we ever want another person to be right, especially when we are arguing to prove our point?

First, my husband was seemingly lying to me, and now God was challenging me too. I still did not want to budge on what I thought was right. Maybe I needed to explain to God what was happening here (as if He did not already know). I replied, "No that can't be; if he is right, then I am wrong, but I know I am right."

In His gentle way, God asked me one more question, "What if I say both of you are right?"

With that question, God immediately stopped me from arguing and shared with me His perspective. In that split second truth, reality hit me hard, allowing me to realize that I could also be wrong, wrong in my attitude. If so, I needed God's grace and His correction. My husband deserves the same grace when he is wrong. My anger and frustration immediately disappeared, and peace overcame me.

It no longer mattered who was right, nor did I remember what we were arguing about. What mattered most was seeking God's forgiveness for my hardened heart and anger. It is the biggest miracle how God can transform us in a split second as soon as the truth is revealed. But we must seek God in prayer so we can grow in this way. There is no condemnation when God whispers, and if we're obedient to Him and allow His whispers to have their humbling effect, then our souls can be transformed. When you are trained by whispers to recognize His presence there is always peace and calmness that transcends your spirit, it's as if it's sinking deep into your bone and through to your marrow. I was able to understand differently and see the beauty in correction.

I thought there was only one option: either I was right, or my husband was right. In my defensiveness, I had doubted the honesty of my husband, and was convinced that I was blameless. I thought that I was the righteous one, and he was a liar. God showed me another way. Perhaps we both genuinely believed we were telling the truth. But the real issue was not who was right; it was an issue of my heart. I had been unwilling to believe the best in my husband, and my pride had kept me from considering that I could be wrong. I was caught in the sin of judging others.

God's whisper was addressing a deeper issue that goes beyond one silly argument. The lesson was this: I do not know everything. Only God sees the depth of our hearts. God used this moment to correct me after I had judged my husband's heart, which is something only He can see. More than that, He corrected the stubbornness of my heart, which was something I was unwilling to see. Having my sin exposed in this way could have made me feel very badly about myself. Instead, the anger and frustration disappeared. His truth freed me and gave me peace and calmness. I was able to ask God's forgiveness for believing I was above making mistakes. And I was able to extend grace to my husband in the same way Jesus extends grace to me. Also, it helped me not to judge others, but to let God be the judge.

Therefore, there is now no condemnation for those who are in Christ Jesus, (Romans 8:1), so even as we face our mistakes, we are not condemned. God is full of grace, and He uses our mistakes to teach us and give us a blessed future. He does it in such a loving way, we are actually able to be grateful for His admonitions and correction. The Lord could have easily whispered just one sentence to me, but instead He showed me three different angles so I could understand. He knows me better than I know myself. How can I doubt or deny the truth? Our Lord wired you and me differently, and He will whisper just the way we each need to hear or to be corrected so we can experience the fullest joy.

Whispers are also prayers. As we whisper to Him in prayer, He will whisper back to us to teach and train us in the path of righteousness. Through whispers we can entertain the presence of the Lord in every moment of life, regardless of our degree of righteousness.

Stay open to correction and give God a chance to transform you. He is the only one who can take away our darkness and replace it with light and peace. Every time I tell this story to others, they all have stories to relate to this. Have you heard whispers of correction before? Did it add peace and calmness to your mind? What do we lose, and how much can we gain? What is He allowing and preparing for us? When we turn to God, we are relying on His steadfast love and truth, and with this conviction, we allow His truth to set us free. Jesus said in John 8:32, *"Then you will know the truth, and the truth will set you free."*

Who Always Knows Best? (Fran)

I'm always interested in stories about marriages. Especially stories with a happy ending. I love 'simple.' Just give me the most simple and direct path to accomplish something and that is what I want. I'll seek to understand it, learn how to repeat it, "make it a habit" you might say, and then I'm happy and on my way.

I know too, that I don't have all the answers. Most of us have areas in our lives where we struggle to stay on course and do the right thing; the thing we know God would want us to be doing. I read the Bible and I pray. I bring issues before the Lord all the time. I've learned so much directly from God. Sometimes He teaches me through the lives of others.

When Pam told me that she had had an amazing experience with her husband, I was especially curious. Her stories are always important. They are honest and true and about the Lord. So, I knew her story would have "a happy ending." I was interested.

I have been married a long time and have experienced the many joys, blessings, and not just a few healed battle wounds. If you are going to have a great marriage, it takes work. Our marriage is like any other, we have both worked at it!

In Pam's story, she explained that she had heard God whisper to her. She had retreated to another room to pray and seek God's help to resolve an argument she was having with her husband. She told God how frustrated she was that Clive was unwilling to admit she was right, and he was wrong. I'm sure that everyone can relate to a situation like this when both parties are determined to defend themselves and their positions. What can you do in a situation like that? How can you resolve that? Pam turned to the Lord for help. Not AFTER the argument, but in the middle of it. What a great example she is!

As I was reading Pam's story, I heard God whispering to me. What I heard Him say was, "It doesn't matter who is right or who is wrong...what matters is that I'M RIGHT."

All of a sudden, it wasn't about who was right about any-thing, what was important to me was what was important to God. In the case of a marriage "discussion" I need to remember whose idea our marriage was...who designed it, planned it, and who has been upholding and providing for us all these years. It's God, and of course I can trust Him to know what's right and what's best.

Why does He whisper to us? Sometimes it's just for us, but most of the time it is also about our relationship with others and our witness for Him in the world. Many of us have heard the saying, "God is good..." and we know to respond, "all the time!" This is also true. "God is right...all the time!" We all can trust Him.

8

OBEDIENCE IS BETTER THAN SACRIFICE

...To obey is better than sacrifice,
and to heed is better than the fat of rams.
1 SAMUEL 15:22B

A Mustard Seed Doctor (Pam)

Years ago, my husband and I were doing annual missions in Guatemala with our church. Our work was to build enclosed stoves for the poor mountain communities. Without them, they had to cook on an open fire. This was dangerous because they were inhaling the harmful smoke and the children would often burn themselves. They were grateful to receive these stoves and we were gratified that we were able to help them.

After several of these trips to Guatemala, I heard God whisper, "I want you to do another mission trip instead." Trusting His voice, and in obedience to God's leadings, I told my husband that I would not be able to go with him to Guatemala in 2013.

I began to look into other missions available at my

church and God said, "NO, NO, NO." Then I looked at nearby churches to see what mission opportunities they offered and again, I heard, "NO, NO, NO." Defeated, I gave up, thinking that these were not whispers from God after all.

Shortly thereafter, one of my friends called to see if I was going to the Order of St. Luke (OSL) National Conference because she needed a ride. I told her that I wasn't interested in going. As soon as I hung up, my Lord whispered, "I want you to drive her, or she will have no way of going." Later I called her back saying I had changed my mind, and that I had even registered myself as a prayer minister for the conference.

At the conference, the main presenter spoke about medical missions they were doing in India under the leadership of a surgeon, Dr. Mike Sabback. He went on to tell how these missions provided medical clinics as well as spiritual teachings and prayer revivals. God whispered, "That's for you." Doubt crept in immediately because they were out of South Carolina and I lived in Texas. At our church, training was required and mandatory. Not only did I not know Dr. Mike, but I wasn't even a member of their church. There were so many obvious obstacles, but because of God's persistent whispers, I knew I had to speak with him.

Emboldened, I caught up with the speaker after his presentation and I told him my desire to go to India with the doctor and serve as a prayer minister. Without hesitation, he encouraged me to connect with Dr. Mike. I was excited, but also nervous about all that could go wrong so I enlisted prayers from my friend for God's good and perfect will to be done. After a month of prayer and waiting, I finally emailed Dr. Mike. He called me right away and accepted my offer to go with him. Once again, I was humbled by God's grace and the power of prayer!

I had no idea about the profound impact partnering with this doctor would have on me, but to this day, it is one of the biggest blessings of my life. In India, we travelled from village to village serving the beautiful people by ministering to their countless physical and spiritual needs. Throughout many parts of the land we taught, prayed, healed, hosted medical clinics where Dr. Mike performed many surgeries. Before this he had a lucrative medical practice in the USA, which he willingly left when God whispered to him to be a servant to people in need. He became my hero and my spiritual mentor, as he was for so many others.

The villagers came to Dr. Mike for all their physical needs, and when there was nothing more he could do, he would send them to us for prayer. With great assurance and confidence, he would tell them, "There is nothing more I can do for you, but what a doctor can't do, God can surely do." Seeing them healed by prayer alone overwhelmed me with joy! There were so many in need and Dr. Mike would never turn down a mother with a baby, even after we closed the medical clinic for the day. He set such an example for all of us as he helped, healed, preached, and taught! We witnessed first-hand what it truly looks like to 'walk by faith, not by sight.' What a beautiful tale of one man, a mustard seed if you will, growing and enlarging God's work here on earth for the good of mankind and for the glory of God.

What if I had not trusted and obeyed the gentle whisper not to go to Guatemala? What if I had not trusted and obeyed the gentle whispers to eliminate all other possible missions? What if I had not trusted and obeyed the gentle whisper, "That's for you," and then emboldened, approached the presenter?

My life and many lives were forever changed by trusting and being obedient to simple whispers. Have you had any whispers or a strong compulsion to do something beyond your understanding? How did you react?

"Instant obedience will teach you more about God than a lifetime of Bible discussions."
—Rick Warren, *The Purpose Driven Life*

"My Plans Cannot Be Thwarted" (Fran)

"This is the design we want for the sanctuary," My husband shared as he was showing a group of men a drawing on a napkin. They were telling us that it wasn't possible. They would try to design it, but they doubted it would work.

I was one of the parishioners chosen to work with the architectural firm the church had selected to design and construct our new sanctuary. We were meeting for the first time. My husband and I had just returned from a tour of English cathedrals and on the flight home David had drawn a floor plan and view of a church; a place we all wanted to reflect and glorify God.

We were surprised, therefore, when the first response we heard from the architectural firm was, "We are sorry, but this design is not possible. It can't be done." Well of course it can, I thought. There are century old cathedrals that were far larger and much taller than the design we were asking for. What followed were many frustrating meetings with the firm who continued to insist that our design was not feasible. We struggled with every option they presented. David believed he had been given a vision and nothing else was satisfactory.

We prayed throughout the whole process that God's will would be accomplished, so in the end we released the design to the architect's plan, trusting that the Lord would recognize that we had done our best. We continued to believe that God had given David the design He wanted months before, but we finally turned it over for God to handle. We believed that God would redeem our mistakes if we had failed Him. So, throughout the many months of construction that followed, we prayed, "Thy will be done!"

Almost two years passed, and the construction phase drew to a close. The day arrived when the scaffolding was to be removed between the upper half of the building and the lower half. It was the first time the arches above would be viewed from the floor.

What? Crisis! Something had gone terribly wrong. The columns and arches had been constructed incorrectly and they did not connect. Word traveled quickly and there was an emergency meeting called. Architects, General Contractor and assistants, the design team, and the leadership teams were contacted. Everyone needed to drop what they were doing and come immediately to convene in the new building!

What had been revealed was that the arches high above, which had been so carefully designed, were not connecting with the column which had been constructed below. This was an extremely serious problem with ramifications impacting the construction schedule, the budget, and the church schedule. What could be a solution to these errors? No one was saying a word. Stunned silence. Who would speak first?

It was my husband. He asked for the contractor's laser arrow and began drawing a line of light. He started up high on one of the upper arches and drew, with light, what was to be the solution. "What if we join this upper section with this lower section... THIS WAY?"

We could see it! It was perfect...and behold, there was

the design from the napkin! We all stood there amazed and some of us in awe! It was beautiful. The construction teams could go back in and sheetrock multilayers of graceful arches that would utilize and blend the differences in the current structure. It would be lovely. The arches would flow, and soar and the space would be beautiful. Everyone immediately understood the solution. Such relief. Such gratitude!

Standing there, that day, in the soon-to-be-finished Sanctuary, I heard God whisper to me. He said firmly, "My plans cannot be thwarted!" And at the same time, I understood, "You can trust ME!" How important are these lessons? All throughout Scripture, one story after another, from the first page of Genesis, through to the last pages of Revelation, these are the themes we learn: God has a plan. His will be done. Trust Him and fear not! Do we have a part? Yes! Pray!! Pray and obey for God's will to be done. Do our best to accomplish His will, and then wait and watch what He will do.

The architects and the construction teams could not explain their mistakes, and only the church design team would understand God's victory! It was an extraordinary time of witnessing a vision, given by God Himself, being accomplished. Despite the plans of men, God's plans will not be thwarted! Worship began that day in His new home!

Go to Him in prayer. Listen and Obey. Trust Him. He will accomplish His plans!

9
I Will Save You

Turn to me and be saved, all you ends of the earth;
for I am God, and there is no other.
Isaiah 45:22

"I Will Save You" (Fran)

I was not expecting this! My whole family was on vacation. It had been planned for over a year and it was supposed to be a time of rest, relaxing, and having fun. Something happened the day before which completely caught me off guard and hit me squarely alongside the head and deeply in my heart!

We all have challenges that continually come up before us even when we think that they have been resolved. This unexpected problem had been years in the making. Hurts I believed had been healed. Questions I thought were resolved. I had seen answers to these prayers in the past and here I was saying them again. So how could this be happening?

"Oh Lord...what am I going to do?"

I was finishing up the morning dishes in the little house

my family had rented for a few days. As I finished whispering these words to God, I watched the dirty, soapy water drain in the sink below me. And then I saw it, and I heard Him whispering gentle words of assurance.

There at the opening of the drain in the bottom of the sink was the most beautiful cross. Where in modern homes today would be a pliable rubber stopper designed to gently catch items you might want to rescue before they washed away, was a beautiful gold and brass cross. Nothing else in the sink shone as brightly under my gaze. It was a beautiful, solid cross stretching across the opening of the drain. Below was the black abyss of an old plumbing system which led to a dark, wet, and surely, nasty sewage system.

As I looked and as I heard...His blessed and familiar peace flowed through me as He whispered to me, "I will save you! Do not be afraid! I will not let you be washed away!" And there He was again, as solid, as faithful, as always.

My circumstances had not changed. The issues were the same, things to be faced and challenges to go through. But it was no longer about my need to manage or have sure footing. It wasn't about a good prayer time, or an understanding of what was going on, because, as He so faithfully reminded me, He was with me, He would help me, He would protect me. He was in charge all the time and I am His.

A Penny for Prayer (Pam)

Do you take time to pick up pennies? They have so little value now that many would not go to the effort to pick them up. My hope is that after reading my story, you might think and act differently!

It was during one of the most difficult times of my

life when I started to pay attention to pennies. It may seem strange, but I found courage and strength from reading the inscription on the penny, "In God we trust." It encouraged me by knowing that all I needed in challenging times was to trust in God. This seemingly simple awareness did not change things for me immediately, but it did allow me to have a living hope so that I could keep on working towards making things better, as written in Philippians 3:13b-14, *Forgetting what is behind and straining toward what is ahead, I press on toward the goal to win the prize for which God has called me heavenward in Christ Jesus.*

When we feel hopeless it can lead to depression and then despair can set in and this is when we can become separated from God. But when we maintain a living hope, it will strengthen and enable us so that we are better able to endure the tough times and thereby do all things for the glory of God.

Recently, during the 2020 Covid pandemic, I was going to visit a friend and get money from the ATM. Because of the shut down from the pandemic, my usual bank was closed, and I heard a gentle whisper, "Just drive around the corner." I did just that thinking there would probably be a working ATM there, but instead I only saw a homeless couple. It appeared they had made that corner their home and they were doing intravenous drugs, right there, out in the open. Usually, I do not give money to homeless people but that day, since I heard a whisper directing me to that corner, I felt led to do something and gave them the little money that I had.

After I returned home, I heard another whisper, "I want you to take them food tomorrow." At first, I was concerned and not sure if it was the right thing to do. I decided to seek counsel from my friend Trog, who helps run a farming ministry for the people who are experiencing homelessness and poverty. I shared what I saw and what God was prompting me to do and I asked him if he felt that was what was best for them? He encouraged me to provide them food as well and give them a printout of some shelters where they could seek help. He cautioned me that while it is a good and a godly thing to help, that they could not really be fully restored unless they were ready to accept that they needed it. Like when Jesus asked the man at the pool of Bethesda, "Do you want to be healed?"

The next day I took them a home cooked meal and the list of resources where they might find help. When I handed them the food, I told them, "I am not going to come back again, but I want you to know that Jesus loves you. If you need help, I've printed out some places where you might be able to get some assistance." They seemed pleased and they thanked me. As I headed back to my car, I noticed a dirty disfigured penny. It was almost unrecognizable, but immediately I picked it up. In this moment, I saw the homeless couple as this disfigured and unwanted penny. I immediately knew God wanted me to pray for them instead of praying for my own gain, and also trust Him to do the rest. How much God loves His creation even when we consider we are unwanted and disfigured by our hurt and pain.

God can do anything without us involved but somehow, He wants us involved in His grander plans. I treasure it as a constant reminder to pray for those two lost souls. I do not understand, nor will I ever know what their future holds, but I trust God called me to pray for them. Now whenever I pick up pennies, it becomes a constant reminder for me to pray for the neglected, abused, unwanted and hurting people as God's calling to intercede for their needs. God's will for us all, is to enjoy the freedom and light of Christ in our living and in our dying.

Can you believe that He hurts when we are hurt? Next time you see a penny, will you pick it up and pray for someone who is in need, as a calling from God? We have a God who does not judge what we have become, but one who sees us as His treasured possession. We do not have to get cleaned up to come before our God as He will meet us wherever we are; even if we're dirty and disfigured like that mangled penny and homeless couple. He created us all in His image and we are all equally important to Him!

Some of you reading this may feel that you are just like that penny. Banged up. Rusted. Marred and scarred by some terrible things that have happened to you or you have done to yourself. God will come to you if you let Him. He will send help to you through other people to give you a chance to turn your life around. God's love and power is sufficient to remove us from wherever we are and give us a future filled with hope and joy. Jeremiah 29:11 says, *"For I know the plans I have for you," declares the Lord, "plans to prosper you and not to harm you, plans to give you hope and a future."* He is waiting with arms opened. I hope you will reach out to him and allow Him to rescue you!

Fran: I wanted to share what I experienced when I first heard Pam's story about the penny. I very seldom find money on the sidewalk or lost in a parking lot. But after I heard Pam tell this story I started to look for coins here and there. In the last two months, I have found a total of 87 cents! They are on the windowsill over my kitchen sink. They remind me to pray for the souls that are lost and need to be found. I hope you start looking for lost coins too.

10

ALL FOR THE GLORY OF GOD

And whatever you do, whether in word or deed,
do it all in the name of the Lord Jesus,
giving thanks to God the Father through Him.
COLOSSIANS 3:17

"I Love You; I Want All of You" (Pam)

My daughter-in-law, Emily and I come from different cultures. We are from opposite ends of the world really, with her being from Minnesota and me from Sri Lanka. We get along so well her friends frequently ask how it is possible when daughters often can't even get along with their own mothers? Several times I may have crossed the line, but she shakes her head and walks away, and I do the same. Our mutual love of God allows us to overcome and get beyond our shortcomings, freeing us to rely on each other's strengths.

I'm grateful for one especially poignant experience that served to greatly deepen and enrich both of our faiths. It happened when God had created a stirring in me, leading me to pray over something that was not right with her.

After praying and not knowing what was wrong, I decided to call Emily to see if she was sick. She assured me that she was fine, but as soon as I hung up God whispered, "She is pregnant." Emily had just given birth to her second child less than a year ago and this news came as quite a shock to me! The next week she called to tell me that she was pregnant with her third child.

During her first trimester she began to bleed and spot. The doctors determined that the source of the bleeding was coming from her uterine wall and that this condition would require strict bed rest. We became quite concerned as it persisted for the next ten weeks. It became more serious as the bleeding increased and was encroaching on the edge of the placenta endangering the baby.

We asked many friends and family and our respective churches to pray! The doctors were at a loss as the bleeding continued. The situation became increasingly serious for Emily and her baby. Would they be okay? It puzzled me and made me wonder why the doctors and prayers weren't able to help reveal a solution. After all, God made this known to me early on, so prayer should be enough to heal her if the doctors couldn't solve it.

Holding on to that confidence, I asked Emily to come and live with me for a couple of weeks so we could pray together. Taking a huge leap of faith, Emily came to Texas with her children for two weeks. Each night after the children went to bed, we both sat together for a time of prayer. One of these evenings she began to open up about some childhood wounds that seemed to haunt her still. We then began to pray more earnestly. As we prayed, Emily started to feel released, becoming more vulnerable, which allowed her to trust more in the process. With this, her deep inner pain was coming to the surface and it was brought out into the open. What a humbling and endearing process this was for us both.

It was in Emily's humility she surrendered her hurt and heart to God and this allowed her to be healed. His love that could now wash over her as she freed herself into his loving and caring arms.

By the 3rd or 4th day, God assured me that she had been healed. However, since it was internal bleeding, it was important to confirm this with a sonogram. The doctors were dumbfounded, but Emily and I knew in our hearts, that it was truly a miracle from God that He had healed her completely! I was relieved that both mother and baby were safe. Not only that, but that baby will never suffer the consequences of the mother's painful past.

After this miraculous healing, I went to God to ask, "Why was prayer alone not enough to heal her physically?" Then, a gentle whisper came to me, "Yes, she could have been healed by prayer alone, but it would have been like putting a band-aid on a gaping wound. I love her and I want all of her."

By this I understood that if our inner wounds aren't addressed and resolved, they could continue to cause harm and hurt us. If we do not bring our wounds before the Cross, they will fester from the inside out. Yes, prayer can reach all those inner wounds through the light of Christ and heal our physical needs. We are made such that our mind, body and spirit are all mysteriously intertwined, and they can and do affect each other.

Since we can't undo our past, our hurts often stay locked up. This can prevent us from dealing with what's really at the root of our troubles and prevent us from being able to be thoroughly healed. When we are ready to fully embrace God, He will carry us through this process, so we are not prisoners of our emotions and hurts. He wants us to experience complete healing, both inside and out, so that we can enjoy His heaven made here on earth. Since God is the same yesterday, today and forever, He can go back to our past and release our emotions associated with hurt. Once freed, we will be able to experience a complete healing of body, mind, and soul.

I asked Emily to share her thoughts with this story.

"If God hadn't healed me, the bleeding could have continued. If it had continued to grow along the uterine wall, underneath the placenta, the placenta would have perished, thereby killing my baby. God knew how to get to my heart and my hurt, as my child was in jeopardy. Because of the damaged placenta, my baby, Gilly, was born 9 days early. I was able to see the 'scar marks' on the placenta after his birth."

God's gentle whispers gave me the confidence to believe that she could be healed by prayer. In obedience to His leading, I invited her to visit, and she agreed to come. It's very important not only to believe but also to obey when God speaks, so that in and through our obedience His good and perfect will can be accomplished for all concerned. Through mine and Emily's faith, trust and obedience, this innocent baby's life was preserved and through God's miracle, our precious grandson Gilead continues to bless us all.

Would you like to enjoy the heaven made on earth for you? What past hurt, pain, guilt or shame would you like to bring before God to surrender and put at the feet of Jesus for a complete healing of body, mind, and soul?

"Slow Down" (Fran)

It was a sunny Sunday morning near a beautiful Florida beach. I was standing next to a woman a little younger than myself. I didn't know her, and I still don't, but I will always remember her. She had just hit my five-year old grandson with her car.

Our family vacation was just beginning. It was Father's Day. We had spent the morning on the beach, and it was lunch time. Some of us were still at the water faucet washing the sand off our feet and off the beach toys, while the rest of the family was spread out across the street and beyond as we headed back to our rented beach house. In an unexpected and impulsive decision, our little grandson, Moses, decided to run across the street to join his cousins. In that split second, we saw the passing car hit him. We saw his little body be thrown high into the air, flipping around and around until he fell and landed in the middle of the road and then lay there lifeless.

I fell to my knees, pleading with the Lord to protect him and save his life. He wasn't moving. My husband ran to him, picked him up and was rocking him firmly as we all gathered around and waited for help, and quietly prayed. Just before the ambulance arrived, his little body stirred and then struggled. He looked up at his grandfather and said, "G-Daddy you are holding me too tight; I can't breathe." The next moment the paramedics were efficiently and gently, putting his little body in the ambulance while his parents squeezed in around him. We stood for a few moments, praying for God's mercy and a miracle. We then shepherded the confused and scared cousins back to the beach house. No one dared say that it was likely that our lives had all changed in those last few minutes...most of all for our precious, little Moses!

Rarely in a situation like this, do you get to speak to the other person involved in an accident. She had been standing next to me as quiet as the rest of us. She turned to me and I'll never forget what she said, "I was on my way home from church. Just before I hit him, I heard the words, "Slow down." My foot was on the brake and I had already begun to slow down when I saw him."

The hospital was close by, so within minutes the nurses and doctors were running tests on Moses that lasted long into the afternoon. Members of the family gathered in the waiting room to continue to pray and support Moses' parents, Tray and Taye. Every testing report came back negative. Could we dare to believe that Moses was going to be ok? Could God, maybe, have rescued him from ALL harm? We all prayed, "Please Lord."

Four hours later, on that blessed Father's Day, little Moses was carried out of the Emergency Room with a popsicle in his mouth and a simple Band-Aid on his left forearm.

Our family really loves Father's Day. We always thank God for the dads in our lives, but the real hero we praise and thank is our Father in Heaven, who saved the life of Moses that Father's Day.

And I will always remember the dear woman who had spent that morning in worship and who was keenly aware and attentive to a loving God who had that day, whispered gently in her ear. After a morning in church, while on her way home, her mind was tuned in to hear the God she loved and knew whisper, "Slow down." He knew what was about to be in my grandson's mind, and what he would do. She heard God's voice and obeyed His whisper, and my grandson's life was saved.

These are common questions which were answered that day:

- Does God see time differently than we do? This story illustrates that He does.
- Does He know when we need protection?
- Does He know what we will be praying for and has a plan to answer us?
- Can we trust Him?

When He whispers to us, He reveals many things about Himself.

Do we know His voice or His promptings?

When He whispers and asks you to do something, and you are sure it is Him, do it! As you can see from my story, sometimes it is vitally important that you respond immediately.

11

It's Not about Me, It's about Him

*The King will reply, 'Truly I tell you,
whatever you did for one of the least of these
brothers and sisters of mine, you did for me.'*
MATTHEW 25:40

Even on Your Best Day (Fran)

"I don't want to go! Not today!" It was Sunday morning. The children and I were expected within the hour. Sometimes I felt like a hypocrite going to church. My four children were finally ready and now it was my turn. I just didn't feel 'good enough' for church. It had been a rough morning until I heard God whisper.

In the Bible I had read about His relationship with me, but what He said that morning, hearing His words whispered to me...I finally understood Him!

If you do exactly what I was doing that morning you will better understand. Hold your right hand up twelve inches in front of your face. Turn your hand facing left and pinch your thumb and forefinger together facing to the left. Now separate your thumb and forefinger exactly ½ inch. I was doing this and was saying, "This is how I feel." That morning I was showing God just how small I felt. It was then He spoke.

He whispered, "Separate your fingers one inch apart." I did it. He said "This is you on your best day! Your worth isn't based on your feelings or behavior. Your worth comes from My Son, Jesus." I understood what He was saying to me. He was reminding me that without Him I am nothing. I need Jesus. I am lost as a sinner but when I believe that Jesus died for my sins, my worth is from Him.

I'm an artist and a woman and I live in a world of emotions. For many years I thought my emotions were the truth tellers...what I felt was what was true. What God was telling me that morning was that my worth to Him, my attendance in church for example, was not to be decided by how I felt about going. What He was telling me in such a simple and obvious way was that whether I felt great or felt terrible, He was waiting for me at church. He wanted me there with Him and with His people. We need each other no matter how we are feeling about ourselves or anything else. Our focus is to be on Him.

But He was telling me more. He was telling me that even on my best day I still wasn't worthy before a righteous God. This may sound harsh and hard. I used to feel that way. I actually love it now because what God showed me is that He loves me no matter what. Good or bad, right, or wrong, He loves me.

It's no longer about me, but it is now ALWAYS about Him! I'm going to church!!!

"Don't Miss Your Biggest Blessing" (Pam)

When I was doing mission work in Guatemala, I learned an important lesson by going to God in prayer. My husband and I went there to help families by building and installing stoves in their homes. My job was to build simple stoves, while my husband did the difficult stoves which required greater skills and took more time. As soon as my project was completed, I would devote my time to the kids by doing crafts, coloring and even playing soccer with them until my husband was done.

We would be dropped off at our assigned location on the mountains and then we walked to the homes of the preselected families in need. All the village kids would follow us wherever we went. One boy stood out to me. His face was covered in dirt and snot and I was instantly filled with love for him. I asked permission from the family to clean him with my wet wipes. I hadn't realized that the village leader saw me caring for the boy. She made a point to tell the team how this touched the hearts of the villagers and brought them joy, as usually the children were neglected. Although it didn't matter to me that anyone recognized my efforts with the children, it did please me to hear of the joy that it brought them all.

Every night, before I sleep, I go to God in prayer on my knees to thank and bless Him for the day. During these prayer times, I also ask God to show me the things that I could've done better but was unaware of due to my ignorance or in my selfishness of preferring my own comfort. On this particular night, my heart was full of joy thanking my Lord for giving me the opportunity to clean that little boy and make a difference in the village. But then a gentle whisper came over my prayer, "You did good, but you missed the biggest blessing and joy to see cleaning Jesus Himself." I was immediately reminded of Matthew 25:40, The King will reply, '*Truly I tell you, whatever you did for one of the least of these brothers and sisters of mine, you did for me.*' I asked my Lord for another chance to clean my Jesus, but I never did get one in Guatemala, but in His grace, He did provide a lot more opportunities in other countries.

Now, when I get to clean the dirty feet of the least of these, I see Jesus. No fear of germs, no bad smells, but only His love and joy poured out of my soul to see Jesus in them. Whether I am with addicts or murderers in prison, there is no condemnation or judgment on my part as I see Jesus in their eyes and every single person becomes important. In this joy, my heart becomes enlarged with an overflowing love of which I didn't even know I was capable before this new awareness! Now I am a different person feeling the joy of the Lord, turning my service to a worship, and I grow strangely dim in the light of His glory and grace. Jesus is with me, in me and before me, and He does the work while I get to enjoy being the feet, hands and mouth of Jesus. There is no greater joy on earth than to be used for His glory!

God used His gentle whispers to further bless, encourage and teach me what it looks like to be humble before Him. We all are subconsciously programmed to do good and right to help others in need, but this new awareness invited me to a higher and fuller depth of love and joy. This new enlightenment was only made possible by faithfully going to God in prayer.

How would you describe your prayer life? Is it a to do list before the Lord or letting God speak to you to bless you with unimaginable moments?

"Wherever God has put you, that is your vocation.
It is not what we do but how much love we put into it."
SAINT TERESA OF CALCUTTA

12

I Am Listening

And if we know that he hears us—whatever we ask—
we know that we have what we asked of him.
1 JOHN 5:15

"It Was Always Her Cross" (Pam)

Back in 2008, I attended a one-day silent retreat. In these retreats, only the leader speaks, guiding and encouraging the participants to be still and enjoy the presence of God in quietness and in prayer. Once we came back together for group time, we could choose to share if we felt led to speak. This is when our leader shared a story about her daughter's cancer.

While Cathy was preparing for her radiation treatment, she removed all her jewelry, including her Jerusalem cross which was a recent gift from her mother. Cathy had come to cherish this cross from the Holy Land and she never took it off. Once her treatment was over, she forgot to grab it before returning to her room. By the time she realized she had left it behind, she rushed back to get it, but her necklace was nowhere to be found! Cathy was heartbroken.

While our leader was sharing this story, I heard a strong internal voice telling me that I was to give my Jerusalem Cross to Cathy. Everything within me was saying, "No, absolutely not!" But this strong internal voice persisted and because it did, I knew it was not from me. Part of me wanted to obey, but the other part of me didn't want to submit. "After all," I told myself, "It's the only thing I have to remind me of my beautiful experiences in Jerusalem." It was also a gift from my husband, so how could I give it to someone else without upsetting him? Especially to someone I don't even know. I am not a person who values jewelry, but whatever I have represents significant times in my life, and this cross was no exception. It reminded me of many special experiences in the Holy Land.

God has taught me that our mind is a battleground. What we feed it, is what it will become. Therefore, we need to feed it with love and the righteousness of God. At this moment I realized my mind was in a battleground. I had to make a choice. Am I willing to feed my desires or obey the voice of God who was speaking to me?

Even after I got back home, this internal voice or it could be said, a strong impulse never left me. I knew I was to let go of my Jerusalem Cross to bless Cathy. Reluctantly, I decided to obey. That Saturday I put my cross into a gift bag and wrote Cathy a letter. I kept it from my husband, knowing that if he asked me why, it would be enough for me to change my mind and keep the cross. On Sunday morning I found Cathy's mom at church and presented her with the gift for her daughter. I quickly left so she couldn't sense my attachment and I could be done with it! Below is my letter to Cathy.

Dear Cathy,

This piece of jewelry is not new, but it has more value added because I was asked to give it to you, to replace the cross you lost in the hospital. I do not own much jewelry, but if I do, it is because there is a special meaning to it. When we visited Israel, my husband bought two Jerusalem crosses; one for me and one for our daughter-in-law. So, I wear this cross as a reminder of my husband's love and care for me. But now onwards, it will remind you of God's love and care for you, as it is His gift to you.

When I had a silent retreat in your Mom's house, she mentioned that you lost your special Jerusalem cross, and immediately my mind told me to replace it with mine. But it was hard at the beginning....so I asked God to let me know if it was His will and give me clarity of mind that I would know for sure. In my next retreat time, I battled with my thoughts and finally came to understand it was His will that I let go of my cross for your joy.

I believe you will be blessed by this cross, not because it came from me, but because it was a gift from God to you. It was blessed by the Bishop when we were in Jerusalem. Please take joy that God loves you very much and you are His special child. When you feel lonely and scared, and the pain crushes your body, hold the cross, and remind yourself of His love, and how close He holds you in His heart. You are His bride, and He will always love you to the very end of the earth. My dear Cathy, this is His gift to you, so be blessed by it.

Love in Christ,
Pam

On that day, I learned the difference between happiness and joy, the joy that comes from Christ. Happiness is temporary, but His Joy is lifelong. When we give or receive something, we become happy, but it will soon be forgotten, and we will feel in need again. But joy is when we give for the glory of God, without any return or expectations; not even receiving the acknowledgement of a thank you! Joy of the Lord satisfies the soul, and we feel deeply satisfied. In such giving, three things happen (it's like three in one); the receiver is benefited, God is glorified, and the joy and peace which passes all understanding is mine (or the giver's).

As soon as I handed over the gift to Cathy's mom, something beautifully transcending happened within me. It's as if I was experiencing a bit of heaven here on earth. When we experience this joy, it is impossible to set our affections on anything other than Him.

Which do you prefer? To be the giver or the receiver? I usually like to be the giver, but I have also had to learn that sometimes we are called to be on the receiving end, so others can be blessed with these sweet blessings from God. It is not required that we have much to be a giver. Like with me, it is only necessary to respond and give from what you have to give. Whether we give from the little we have or from our surplus, we can point to Jesus in our giving and receiving, and then God will be glorified.

Record your joys in giving and in receiving. Consciously analyze and see which has made a more powerful impact in your life?

Crosses in the Judean Wilderness (Fran)

After a half hour of winding our way carefully on the narrow and rocky road, our bus stopped, and our class unloaded. We gathered around our instructor for the brief teaching he would give us before we would be released for a time of quiet reflection. We were in the middle of the Judean wilderness in Israel. It was the same wilderness where Jesus spent forty days wandering by Himself. As I looked out across the miles and miles of barren and dusty landscape, I was suddenly impressed with the image of Christ wandering for days unnoticed and alone. It became so real and seemed totally possible.

Gazing off into the horizon as our professor was talking, I gradually began to discern a remarkably simple black cross far off on the crown of one of the distant hills. I wondered if I was imagining it until I began to see another cross, and then another. I wondered why? They appeared to be in a row. What could that mean?

When our professor finished speaking, I asked Him what the crosses were for. He responded that they were put there many years before for pilgrims. "It's easy to get confused and lost out here. If a traveler follows from one cross to another he will eventually be led to safety and shelter." I loved that image then and I love it still to this day.

Since that day, I have looked for crosses wherever I am. And I find them! It has become a theme for my life. I am always looking for crosses and every time I see one, I hear God's whispers, "I am with you," and "Follow Me," and "I will show you the way." They are whispers of encouragement and comfort. Words of love and faithfulness. Maybe you don't need reminders of His love and presence, but if you ever do, look for crosses and think of Him!

13

BE MY HANDS AND FEET

Very truly I tell you, whoever believes in me
will do the works I have been doing,
and they will do even greater things than these,
because I am going to the Father.

JOHN 14:12

Be a Witness in All Things (Fran)

Along with a small group of people, I had been selected to work on the design for the new church sanctuary. I know we all felt the same way. None of us expected or aspired to have such an enormous opportunity. We each resolved to do our best. The passion I personally brought to the table was simply to proclaim The Gospel everyplace possible. Everything must point to Jesus and His cross. The Sanctuary must proclaim, "This is a HOLY place. Jesus is here!"

The very first decision was to embrace the cruciform shape, meaning a cross. It is a traditional plan chosen for many historic churches, large and small. There were hundreds of decisions to be made during the process, but what

I considered with every design was: "Can a cross be integrated into this item?" Consequently, today you will see that there are crosses in the window frames, in the railings, above the altar, in the lights, in the design of the carpet, everywhere possible. The front doors themselves are a large cross on glass doors. The doors are designed so that the large cross is divided down the middle of the doors and the brass handles, designed to be part of the cross, are used to open the cross. This is meant to visually and physically remind each person entering the building that the way into God's Kingdom is through the cross. There is not a place you can sit or go in the building where you cannot see a cross. You cannot help but be reminded that Jesus is with us. Our hope is that when people enter the Sanctuary, they hear God whisper, "You are now in My home. I am here!" And what I learned is that even a building can tell His story.

My part on the design committee was to obey God's whisper, "Proclaim the Gospel." I've come to understand that He wasn't asking me to be a witness only in the designing of the sanctuary, but in my whole life. I watch for His witnessing to me, and I seek to be a witness for Him. I have come to understand that often it begins with a whisper from Him.

Overcome with the Love of Jesus (Pam)
Out of hundreds of miracles I have personally witnessed and participated in while in India, there is one about a little boy that I keep close to my heart. Ever since becoming a grandma, I am deeply touched by little children.

On a previous mission trip, God had healed a man as I was praying over him and casting out demons, and now, this time his wife brought her two-year-old nephew to me for healing. He had severely injured his thumb in a door jam. It had been broken over a year ago and it had healed at a right angle, causing him great pain if he used it. Because of the debilitating pain, the boy only used his left hand and would not allow anyone to touch his broken hand. I asked this faithful woman to write a short note describing the situation with her nephew and it went as follows:

"Doctor had given him an injection to ease the pain and to get the finger straightened up, but nothing has happened. Then the second injection was given, but nothing happened. Doctor said to do the operation, but my brother said no. I told him about you, that the prayer team is coming, and please bring your son here. Your son will be absolutely fine."

After we finished teaching that day, they brought the boy to me. He was very frightened, and he wouldn't even allow me to take a look at his finger. In light of his resistance, I decided to anoint his head with oil and pray over him, and soon he fell into a deep sleep. I was then able to look at his right hand. In seeing how it was fixed at a right angle and knowing he was living in pain, my heart filled with sadness and I was overcome with the love of Jesus for this little child. In this moment, I heard a very distinct whisper creating in me a strong compulsion that I mindlessly obeyed. I am sure that you have had strong compulsions to do something good for someone and because you recognize that it's beyond your imagination you realize that it is from God. In these instances, there is no need of confirmation, so you just do it.

Right then I took his right hand and sucked the thumb. Even though he was in a deep sleep, he still felt the pain from me touching it. He grunted in pain and pulled his finger out of my mouth. To our amazement, this boy's thumb was now nearly straight and only slightly crooked!

While the child was still asleep, I put his thumb back into my mouth and sucked it once more. After this, it was now perfectly normal. We were all filled with awe in seeing the power of a living God and we all gave praises to Him!

When I returned to my group and shared what an amazing miracle God did in this little boy's life, someone blurted out, "Yuck, what made you think that you should put his finger in your mouth?" If God created this world and God has whispered to me, why should I be afraid of the germs of the world? It dawned on me that when I am praying and helping people, I only see Jesus and what He wants me to do.

On another occasion when I was in China. While in the restroom, there was a woman who had fallen in the toilet in the adjacent stall and she was shouting for help. These were not traditional toilets, so squatting was required. Hearing her cry for help I ran to her stall and saw this poor elderly woman on the floor with her cane beside her and unable to get up. I helped her up and made a toilet seat with my legs for her to sit. Again, everyone wanted to know if I was sprayed while helping her? Honestly, I had no idea. I don't remember what happened, but what I do remember is that my heart was full of love for Jesus and grateful that I was in the right place at the right time to aid someone in their time of need.

Sometimes God puts you in a place to be of help to others. It is not for you to feel great, or for you to feel yucky, but for you to have the chance to be the hands and feet of Jesus to others. When presented with these God-ordained opportunities, it will fill you with such joy, that you will not think about the circumstances. It's as if you cease to exist and only peace and joy sustain you in your actions.

Have you ever had strong compulsions to help others?

I also consider these whispers from God. God might not call you to fix fingers or make a body toilet for others but be open and be ready to say, 'Yes' to whatever you feel strongly called or led to do. When you are called to do something good for the sake of others, just do it anyway, and it will become second nature as you continue to answer God's call to serve Him by serving others.

14

HELP MY UNBELIEF

I do believe; help me overcome my unbelief!
MARK 9:24

I Still Choose to Pray for Him (Pam)

The Bible tells us that God speaks to us through visions and dreams. Do you believe that God would speak to you this way? I didn't really, but the Lord changed my unbelief through a series of experiences. I soon became a believer in His ways and in His reliability.

It tells us in the Bible that God spoke and guided many people through their dreams. My favorite is how God instructed Jesus' father, Joseph. It was through his dreams that he was guided by God to take Mary as his wife. Through many of my own experiences, I have learned to discern, and I have come to trust in God's whispers through my dreams.

About twenty years ago I had a rather memorable dream. I saw the earth dividing and in the middle of it was a fiery lake. I was on one side and someone very dear to my heart was on the other side. I reached out, grasping, trying to pull him to me, to my side of the lake. It was so unsettling; it woke me up. I had a feeling of fear that was running through my entire body, as if it had really happened! These kinds of dreams, where I feel as if I've actually lived them, are rather dramatic experiences for me. Because they are so visceral, I refer to these types of dreams as my living dreams. With this dream, I was having trouble discerning any meaningful or real life connection, so I chose to put it out of my mind.

Then a week later, I had the exact same dream. My loved one was on the other side of the fiery lake and I tried to reach for him and pull him to me. Like the last time, I woke up in fear, a palpable fear coursing throughout my body. It puzzled me, but I still put it aside as I was unable to make any sense of it.

When I had the same dream again, I woke up wondering and worrying that my dear one was in the wrong place at the wrong time. I was now greatly concerned for him, so I called him to share my recurring dream. As I did, I warned him and encouraged him to be careful! Now that I had cautioned him and because he thanked me, I felt relieved and released myself from further worry or concern. It wouldn't be until years later that I would discover the real meaning of my dream, and what he later shared with me was truly 'a time of darkness in his life.'

Before I came to understand my dream, the dark side of his life became public. He asked me to overlook a sinful situation. When I refused to go along and instead stand for the biblical truth, he became annoyed. In fact, because of my conviction to stand strong and not compromise myself, he told me to never speak to him again. In his own words, he firmly stated, "That according to your Bible, I should consider him as dead." Of course, I was terribly disheartened by his reaction, but I agreed to go along with his wishes.

It was very discouraging to be so disconnected from him, especially not knowing how long the situation would persist without reconciliation. I was concerned that he would not hear or see the truth of the matter, especially in a world where his sin was so readily overlooked and even considered acceptable. No matter how hurt I was, I still chose to pray for him. Always, I turn to prayer when I do not know how to handle a situation or a person.

A few years later, he called to thank me for sharing my dream and standing strong on my convictions. He informed me that back then he was living against God's best for him. In fact, he continued to tell me that he was living in complete sin and that hell would have been a suitable place for him. In that moment, my heart leaped for joy! I quickly reassured him that we all are sinners, including myself, and that no sin is too big for God's grace and forgiveness. I went on to remind him that God does not judge us nor keep a record of our past as in Psalm 103:12, *As far as the east is from the west, so far has he removed our transgressions from us.*

What if I had not chosen to reach out in love to share my disturbing dream? What if I had given in to the lies and not stood strong in my conviction of biblical truth? How then would he have had the chance to accept the Truth when the world accepted the easy way out? God's truth now allows him to live more fully in the joy and freedom of our loving God. It wasn't the dream that provoked him to change, but it was a combination of both the dream and my determination not to accept the sin as good and right.

He gradually began to change his life! Now he is a new creation through Christ Jesus, enjoying the light of Christ and helping so many people in need. This is a wonderful testimony proving the depth, breadth and reach of God's faithfulness, forgiveness, and grace. When He loves and works in us, it is not for our benefit alone, but it is for the benefit of many! Until this experience, I hadn't truly realized how God wants us to be in cooperation doing His work and that He engages us to be used in the lives of others. He uses us and our relationships with others to accomplish His work.

Every dream is not a living dream, but when I wake up feeling those emotions as if I have lived them in that moment, I now pay attention and begin to pray over them. When the same dream keeps returning, I have learned, through trusting His Spirit in me, to communicate what He has shown to me in a loving Christ-like way to whoever is involved.

Please write down in the pages provided in the back of this book any living dreams you have had. Please pray over them or over the person in the dream.

"I Can Deal with Distractions" (Fran)

It was our first Christmas with my family in New York. Traveling all day with two little children and a three-month old infant was quite an ordeal, but we had finally put them to bed and things were quiet. It was then my mother told us, "I have a doctor's appointment in the morning." She had my attention, and I was no longer aware of my exhaustion.

"The doctors have found a tumor and we are planning the surgery to remove it," she explained.

"Are they sure Mom?" I asked her as she hadn't mentioned any of this when we were home in Texas.

"This will be my third doctor to see and only to confirm that I'm ready for the surgery. The tumor is apparently the size of a grapefruit."

My husband's immediate response was to ask, "Can we pray for you Mom?" David and I both knew that turning to God in prayer, asking for His guidance and protection and His healing, was what she truly needed. Prayer was our best response!

My mom would not normally have felt comfortable with us praying for her but in this situation she and my stepdad were both understandably open to sharing their uncertainty and fear. We stood around her in the kitchen, lovingly placed our hands on her, bowed our heads and David began to pray. It was quiet as he began, and it felt like a holy moment calling on God to join us.

As soon as David started praying, my trained mother's ears began to hear sounds coming from the guest room at the end of the hall. FOMO...every child has this condition wired into them. "Fear of Missing Out." Just as David started praying our precious children started calling out for me. "Mommy, can you come here...Mommy? Mommy?!"

"Good grief, not now," I thought, immediately distracted. I consoled myself thinking that they would stop and that they wouldn't hear us and fall back asleep. I tried to refocus. Back to the prayer. Back to God. I heard myself saying to God, "Don't mind them God, the kids are fine, let's focus on this prayer of healing my mom."

But the children didn't stop calling out. I became so concerned that God was distracted too. Had He missed the family's plea to heal my mom? I slipped away from the circle around my mom and hurried to quiet the kids and spent my time with them praying that God had heard our prayers despite the noise and distractions. How could He have heard us. It was a restless night, wondering what the doctor would find and what the process would mean for my mom.

The next morning my mom and stepdad returned from her doctor's appointment elated. The tumor was gone! Totally gone! What apparently had been so advanced and easy to find was no longer there. It was then I heard God whisper to me, "When my people pray, I AM there" and "There will always be things going on in the world around you...I can multitask!" Noise and distractions have never bothered me since!

God healed my mom that Christmas. He graciously answered our prayers and performed a miracle! I wish I could tell you that my mom became a devout believer from that experience, but she didn't. The person whose faith was deepened that day was mine! And His whisper to me revealed a great deal about Him.

Here is a list of questions many of us have asked:

- Do we think He hears our prayers?

- Do we think He gets distracted when listening to us?

- Do we think God is disinterested or too busy for our concerns?

- Do we question whether He really does heal today?

His answers:

- "I hear your prayers."

- "I don't ever get distracted when you are praying."

- "I DO heal today!"

- "I AM always here!"

- "I whisper because I love you."

Since then, I have never questioned or been concerned about the environment surrounding people who are seeking God's presence in prayer. And I have never questioned whether He will answer my prayers. I don't always know how He will answer them. When I pray, I bring before God my concern or request, but then my heart's desire is to trust Him and the answer He knows is best. I surrender my desires for His desires. I trust Him and He has shown me that I can!

15

BURDEN OF UNFORGIVENESS

Do not judge, and you will not be judged.
Do not condemn, and you will not be condemned.
Forgive, and you will be forgiven.
LUKE 6:37

Burdened by Unforgiveness (Fran)

How many times have you heard about the need to forgive? Perhaps you have read about the importance of forgiving. Maybe you have listened to sermons about it. Can you remember all the times you have had discussions in your mind about a person who has hurt you?

Have you ever said The Lord's Prayer and choked a little when you came to the line, *Forgive us our sins, for we also forgive everyone who sins against us?* My voice instinctively softens when I get to that line and I'll take a quick detour in my heart and think to myself, "What does that really mean? Surely God isn't thinking about my need to forgive 'so-and-so'?" OR "Surely He doesn't mean it!" My husband David has a saying about forgiveness, or rather unforgiveness, which is the poison you drink when you're hoping it is for someone else! How important, even dangerous, is it to not forgive others in our lives?

The year our oldest son Jed, was graduating from High School, the leadership of the school came to my husband and asked him to give the Baccalaureate speech. He jumped at the chance to speak some words of wisdom into the minds of this wonderful group of young, clueless adults. Thinking about what topic would be the most important lesson these kids needed to hear, and to best equip them for their future, David chose forgiveness.

As I heard David unpack this lesson before the student body, I began to pray that their parents were listening too. I knew we are never too old to hear a teaching on 'forgiveness.' Surely there were adults present that night struggling with the need to forgive! God commands us to forgive. Why is that?

This is a story that happened in my family. It happened between my mom and dad. It happened to my mom. I know it is a tragic story that all too quietly burdened and hurt my mother's life. The real tragedy is that she did it to herself.

I had come home to attend my dad's funeral. I was staying with my mom and stepdad. Sometimes during the quiet moments around an event like a funeral, people are aware of something within them that finds its way to the surface of their emotions and in a moment of fatigue, grief, or relief, they open up and share it. During this visit my mom shared something about her life which I had never known.

My mom had been living a life, a wonderful life, but with a dark and debilitating secret she had been protecting. She was in a second marriage to a man who adored her and had for over twenty years. They both had healthy, grown married kids leading productive lives. They had lots of grandkids who adored them. Their lives were full and blessed. I was happy for them and admired them in so many ways.

So, I was stunned and sad for her when she, in a moment of candor and grieving, shared with me that shortly after she heard of my dad's death, she sought time alone to cry. She was realizing that she would be unable to forgive my father face-to-face. She had been harboring anger and unforgiveness towards a person who years before had been unfaithful to her in their marriage. She had been angry and unforgiving for over thirty years and now he was gone. She had thought she was somehow hurting him by withholding her forgiveness, when truly she was the one being controlled and the one hurting. I looked at her and I was overwhelmed with sadness for her as I understood what she was telling me. Then I heard God whisper, "Don't live a life of unforgiveness. Forgive quickly. You can give to Me whatever hurts you." He wants us to forgive and give up burdens, so He will help us! He did, in fact, try to help my mom.

Only months before, as God would arrange it, both my mom and dad were sick at the same time, in the same hospital! My father heard that my mom was there, so he managed to get a wheelchair and find his way to her room. He had a mission and was determined to talk with her. I know she must have been surprised to see Him, but perhaps even more surprised, to hear what he said. After almost twenty-five years he asked for her forgiveness. In his wheelchair and at her bedside, he faced his wounded wife from years before and asked her to forgive him. He told her how sorry he was for all the pain he had caused her those many years before. He was seeking forgiveness and healing. I know my mom was surprised and was unprepared and unwilling. She refused to forgive him. She refused!

I have reflected so often on this story. It has caused me great sadness to think that after so many years of blessing and goodness and love, my mom had privately chosen to cling to the hurt, anger, and bitterness of her past. So how do we find healing and release and enjoy God's peace? Turn to God in prayer and ask for His help. He is always looking for ways to help us, to encourage us, to teach us, and give us opportunities to trust Him and grow closer to Him.

Liquid Love of God (Pam)

Forgiveness is one of my favorite topics to cover during mentorship. Largely, because unforgiveness can be as corrosive as a cancer growing inside, and when we are unable to forgive, we are preventing ourselves from enjoying the fullness of life that God wants for us. You are not completely free until you forgive others, not because they deserve it, but because you deserve to live in freedom. Forgiveness is not denying the hurt that happened or forgetting about it. However, forgiveness is a choice we make and sometimes we might need divine help, God's graces, to fully let go of the past and rest in His presence.

One of my all-time favorite stories of forgiveness was when I was asked to pray over a person who was terminally ill and was not expected to live much longer. I asked God (that's my prayer whispers to Him), "How and what am I to pray over him?" God whispered back to me, "Ask about the unforgiveness in his life, and then ask about his relationship with his dad." Now that I had a direction for prayer, I was encouraged and emboldened to proceed!

Knowing the part of the city I needed to go to was dangerous, I felt it wise to invite a friend to accompany me as I ventured to this man's neighborhood to pray for him. My friend gladly accepted, and we met up and went together to the place where we could all be together to pray. When we arrived, we were greeted by him and his friends and as we sat there, they waited for me to initiate the prayer. I began by saying, "Before I came here, I prayed to my God and I was given two questions to ask. I will pray only after the two questions." Then I turned to the sick man and asked, "Is there any unforgiveness in your heart?" He replied "No, I am fine." I waited quietly so that he might search his soul and think more deeply about his past. One of the leaders of this group spoke up, sharing that he was asked this same question before and in haste, he had replied in kind, but eventually realized he had harbored feelings of unforgiveness about his wife who had died. It was then that this sick man started to cry and share his own story.

This man's wife had left him for another man and one day in a rage, he bought a gun and went to his ex-wife's house intending to kill her. He held the gun out, ready to shoot, but he could not pull the trigger. In hindsight, he now believes that God prevented him from killing his wife which saved him from a life in prison. He admitted that he had never forgiven her. I explained why forgiveness was absolutely necessary for his inner healing and physical healing.

Once he understood the destructive power of unforgiveness and the beauty in the freedom of forgiving, I asked him my second question. "How is your relationship with your dad?" Again, he started to sob. His dad had died and as far back as he could remember, his dad was in and out of jail, making it impossible for the kind of relationship he had desired to have with him. Immediately, God allowed me to know in my heart to choose a man from the crowd and appoint him as the dad and get the sick man to tell everything he would have wanted to tell his own father.

Obeying God's direction, I asked the appointed dad to give his 'adopted' son the blessing of his love and the acceptance of a father. When the blessing was being poured over him and the terminally ill man was hearing how much he was cared for by his father figure, he continued to cry and was released and was no longer able to talk. With this, all the other men started to gather around him crying out loud, sharing the love of our Father, God. I have never before seen men crying out loud like this. There was not a dry eye in the room!

We were all aware of a powerful wave moving, making the entire house feel hot and full of the divine Father's Love. The entire atmosphere was changed, and it was as though we could actually touch God, fully feeling His presence. Everything changed and everyone was transformed in this moment. It was as if the same current of electricity went through all of us at the same time, connecting us and energizing us with His love. Even though I have witnessed many miracles with forgiveness, I had never experienced God's love this way; the power of what I now refer to as the liquid love of God! Without me having to pray over this man's illness, God began healing him spiritually and emotionally, even though his physical body still suffered. It is God's love that heals us from inside out; however, unforgiveness will block the love from flowing through us. When someone can release unforgiveness in the heart, there is often a physical healing too.

I believe forgiveness to be a fourfold event:

1. Forgive the other person. Not because they deserve it, but because you deserve to live in freedom.

2. Forgive yourself. This is the unknown factor for many, but do it anyway, so you can enjoy freedom and healing.

a. How can you forgive yourself? We are not fully able to accomplish this on our own, but God will do it for you when you turn to Him and ask His help. It's a divine act of love.

b. Why is it important? This cuts our ties to any darkness created by harboring anger, guilt, or shame that could separate us from a pure and holy God.

3. Pray for them, the offender, the one who did you wrong. This is hardest for many but do it anyway. You never know what God has in store for them or even for you, through your prayers. Perhaps they might come to repent!

4. Help them if they are in need. Many have asked me the question: "How do I know if I have truly forgiven the other person, especially when the memory still lingers?" I answer them by telling them that when you are willing and ready to help them, you will know that the pain no longer controls you, but that you now have a choice and in making that choice, you will be freed.

Do a soul search to see if there is any hint of unforgiveness in your life? Invite Jesus into these wounds, as only He can heal your heart. Then you will be able to forgive the offender with His help and the past will not control you. Instead, you will be free.

16

𝓘 𝓗AVE 𝓟LANS FOR 𝓨OU

For I know the plans I have for you," declares the Lord,
"Plans to prosper you and not to harm you,
plans to give you hope and a future.
JEREMIAH 29:11

Initiating a Chorus of Prayer (Pam)

This is my story of how God can guide us in visions to do good to others for His glory alone. This same story can also be found in the first chapter of *Night Light,* a book written by the gentleman in my vision, Joseph Acton.

In September 2016, while I was praying on my knees, I could see a man in agonizing pain, holding onto his chest. When I have these types of visions while praying, it's as if I'm 'seeing with my spiritual eyes.' He was not someone I knew well by any measure. I had seen this man only twice before in passing, and it was several years ago. I knew him as Josh, an Anglican priest, and the Director of a healing ministry, the Order of St. Luke (OSL). He resided in California and was a well-known guest speaker and prayer Director at the OSL national conferences I had attended years before.

Now I have been trained to recognize when my visions, my 'seeing with spiritual eyes', are insights from God, as opposed to something I've conjured up on my own. God was calling me to pray for Josh, for whatever he was going through. As I was praying, I heard a gentle whisper, "Tell him, it will bless him!" How could I? I barely know him! What if he thinks I'm some sort of crazy person? I did not know where to begin, but I have learned over the years that God is reliable and so I trust when God tells me to do something, I must obey. He always provides the way, as in 1 Samuel 15:22b, *To obey is better than sacrifice, and to heed is better than the fat of rams.* So regardless of my discomfort and possible embarrassment, I pressed on, not worrying about what he might think, because within my heart, I knew I only wanted God to be glorified.

In obedience to this calling from God, I prayed daily for Josh. Meanwhile, I was able to secure his email address so I could reach out to him. Knowing and trusting in this man's godliness, and in obedience to God's prompting, I was emboldened to retell my vision of his agonizing pain and how God had brought him to me and instructed me to pray for him daily.

Then two months later, I learned that he had suffered a massive heart attack while driving to the airport for an OSL conference. By some miracle, his car seemed to steer itself and to his complete amazement he saw a hospital right on the corner! He made it to the parking lot and while trying to enter, he fell onto the pavement in excruciating pain.

Thank goodness a nurse spotted him and rushed out to drag Josh into the emergency room. Josh most likely would have died had that nurse not been there just at that time. After an EKG, the physician's assistant chose to order a sonogram. This was not standard protocol, but the sonogram technician chose to fulfill the PA's request and scan Josh's heart anyway. While scanning, a cardiologist was walking in and noticed Josh's heart on the screen. He quickly yelled, "Code Stemi!" meaning that the patient needed a stent immediately!

So many things had to happen for Josh to survive his massive heart attack. As he recounts in his book "Night Light" (page14):

"Had I missed the off-ramp, in all likelihood, I would have died. Had I not pulled into the road where the regional cardiac center was, I would have died. Had I not had that powerful little nurse respond to me in the darkness of that parking lot, I would have died. If not for Brian (sonogram tech) breaking the rules or for Dr. Ho (Cardiologist) deciding to change his routine, I would have died. But when I thank God for His miraculous intervention, I thank Him first for the woman who prayed consistently for two months prior to my heart attack, and all because she was obedient to a vision. I believe and know in my heart and soul, that her actions initiated a 'chorus of prayer' that laid the track for all these miracles to occur."

He went on to tell readers that his type of heart attack is referred to as a 'widow maker,' meaning most people do NOT survive it! Even more astounding, the estimated time that his heart attack went untreated was almost forty minutes and by any typical medical standards, Josh should have died!

Did you know that in the New Testament of the Bible, the Book of Revelation about end times was given to the apostle John through a vision? If our God of creation can speak to the people in the Bible who were willing to hear and listen, why wouldn't He do it with us? I now know that God does do this with us. Will we respond in the same way if God comes to us like this? I pray we do!

"I Will Tell You through David" (Fran)

It was unmistakable. Not impossible, I thought, but definitely unmistakable. I had heard Him. And I knew it. To document it in real time, I leaned over to tell Debbie, a good friend, what I had just heard. She leaned closer as she knew I wanted to tell her something. I had to practically yell but no one around us cared. I yelled, "I just heard God speak to me and He told me, 'What I want you to do, I will tell you through David!'" She smiled at me, but I'm not even sure she heard me.

We were standing in a large room filled with women. We were singing as loudly as we could, praising a God we loved! It was a Women's Retreat at a rustic campsite in the middle of Arkansas. Summer and hot, we didn't care. We were inside a rustic camp building and the fans were blowing and the music was blaring. We could sing as loud as we wanted and the louder, the better. We were praising the Lord.

That was the setting when He chose to whisper to me, "What I want you to do, I will tell you through David!" You might ask, "How did you hear Him with all the loud music and singing?" I don't know, but I heard Him loud and clear, as if I was alone in a quiet place. That is comforting to know, isn't it? We often think we need to be in a nice quiet spot to listen for God, but I can assure you, that if God wants to tell you something, He can and will!

The retreat continued through the weekend and His words to me got lost in all the other things I was experiencing and learning. The whole group of us got home from the retreat on Sunday afternoon. I was in our bedroom unpacking and telling David about the fun, the teaching and all the things I could remember. He appeared to be interested, but in the middle of my sharing, he grew quiet. I noticed and asked him what he was thinking about. He looked at me seriously, and I knew it was important, so I focused on his face. He said, "Would you consider becoming the Small Group Minister at the church?" I studied his face and saw he wasn't kidding. So, I thought for a moment and answered him back seriously, "No way!"

Truly I had always done what David asked me to do. We were church planters, all hands-on deck. I was always willing to help him and support the new church. But the thought of taking on the leadership of one of the important ministries was well beyond my imagination! I got back to my unpacking and he asked again, "Please reconsider."

God graciously reminded me of His whisper and added, "Remember what I said?" Now I was rethinking what David had asked...and my immediate answer.

Then I recalled a letter David had recently brought home from a woman on staff at the church. She had written to him but asked him to share her words with me. He read it to me and in it she thanked me for the way I had ministered to her. She told David in her note that she was grateful for me and how I had helped her.

I started putting together the pieces that God was giving me. He was wanting me to understand that He was serious about His message and David's request. God was confirming for me that He knew I could do the job as Small Group Minister and that it was His idea. I knew He wanted me to succeed and would help me. Returning to David's question, I now knew what the right answer was, and the purpose of God's whisper on the retreat. I knew what I had to do.

I have a reputation with my grandkids...I'm proud of it actually. I have been working on this way of living long before they were born. It is a well-developed part of my faith journey and my relationship with God. I'm talking about the Greek word 'Metanoia.' It means: To go in the other direction. My translation is 'Repent.' My grandkids have come to call me "U-TURN GIGI." I always smile when with a car full of kids, I miss the turn and everyone screams and yells, U-TURN, GIGI!" I look for the first and quickest place to turn around and correct my way. Metanoia!

I was on a mission...to find my husband David and set the record straight. I found him and without pausing I said, "If the position for the Small Group Minister is still available, my answer is now, 'Yes.'" The position was not filled of course, and I became the Small Group Minister at our church. I was a great SG Leader. Do you know why? Guess who was actually leading the way and calling the shots? You are right, it wasn't me. It was "U-TURN GIGI" under the direction of a mighty and loving God who continued to direct me; a God who kept me on track with His many whispers! He was faithful, as always is His nature.

When you hear God whisper to you, don't overlook the opportunity to consider all the arrangements He often has made to provide for you. All the things He has done to confirm for you, so you know without question, that it wasn't a human idea! It was His idea. Because He has plans for each of us. In Jeremiah 29:11 says, *"For I know the plans I have for you...."*. We have a purpose. We have jobs to do for Him.

But what we ultimately need to know is that He has a big plan, a plan to save His people, and His plans just happen to always include us.

Special advice: Get used to "U-TURNS!" We all have to make them! If you get off track, make a mistake, overshoot your turn, or even intentionally turn one direction when He has asked you to turn the other...'Metanoia', dear friend! Repent! Get back on the right road as soon as you can! The safe road to be on is the one with Him. The one He called you to and prepared for you!

17

LIVING FOR THE GLORY OF GOD

So whether you eat or drink or whatever you do,
do it all for the glory of God.
1 CORINTHIANS 10:31

It's Good to Create Things Just for Me (Fran)
It was my first visit to England, and I was standing in a historic and beautiful cathedral. It was filled with art that represented ideas and images that spoke of faith. Our guide had turned our attention to the decorated ceiling seventy feet above us. He was describing a boss. A cathedral boss is a decoration positioned where the arches meet. They are always located at the very highest part of the ceiling. In this cathedral each boss was unique and had been designed to tell a story from the Bible. Our whole group was struggling to see what was being described by our guide.

Finally, someone in our group voiced the complaint that was on everyone's mind. "I can't see what you are talking about!" Our guide turned around to face us and calmly repeated a story he had told to many visitors before us and the story's lesson is one of timeless relevance and importance.

123

He began, "Centuries ago one of the original sculptors for the cathedral was leading a patron on a tour of the cathedral. There was much to see and explain. They came to the center of the sanctuary and the artist pointed to the beautiful, vaulted ceiling above them. He began to explain in detail about a particular image of which he was especially fond. Standing at his side, straining, and squinting, the patron finally expressed his frustration. The patron was unable to see anything the artist was describing. The cathedral artist turned to the patron and respectfully and reverently said, "I didn't make it for you." The cathedral artist had created his work knowing that no one would ever see it, except God."

As our guide finished his story from centuries ago, I also heard God whisper to me that day, "It's good to create things just for Me."

I'm an artist and whenever I am beginning a piece of work, I always have in mind who I am making it for. Sometimes it's just for me, sometimes it's for someone else and occasionally it's for money. These used to be good reasons, but I'll tell you what has become the most important purpose for me now. Now I create my artwork as if I was creating it only for God. I pray before I start that what I would create would please Him. I pray as I work, asking for His guidance so He will be pleased. I pray when I'm finished asking if He is pleased.

This story and the artist's words have been retold throughout the centuries and, I imagine into the hearts of countless believers. How many millions of Christians live their lives like this obscure and unnamed artist, faithfully and quietly, serving a magnificent God, who sees, and understands, and appreciates. How many of us work and work and offer our best every day and as much as we can, live our lives for God? How many people around the world would want to know that there is a God who sees their work, understands their sacrifice, and values what they do? God showed me that day, through the story of the cathedral boss, that He sees these things, and they are of value to Him...maybe to Him alone!

Full on an Empty Stomach (Pam)

I returned home from a two-week trip to China with severe pain in my right heel. I had developed a very painful condition known as Plantar Fasciitis. I learned from the doctor that if the pain did not go away, I would require surgery. I couldn't walk without pain, and by the end of the day, I needed to rest my foot on a bag of ice and do several foot exercises to cope with the debilitating discomfort.

I had gained five pounds while in China! I wondered if the additional weight might be aggravating the problem. I reasoned that if I lost the weight, it would help to alleviate the pressure on my foot and reduce my acute pain. So, I set out to lose weight and since I wanted to lose it quickly, I decided to try fasting as a means of losing the extra pounds.

I was familiar with fasting from previous Lenten disciplines. So, I began. I set out to fast as much as I could to achieve my desired weight, but my weight would not budge. Ultimately, I gave up and I accepted the fact that I would have to live with the pain, the extra weight, the ice bags, and trust God to do the rest.

Every day I would step on our bathroom scale to see if I was winning the battle. I took note of my pounds and their ups and downs almost daily. Sometimes I looked forward to these daily weigh-ins; and other times I did not. Often, I would step on the scale twice a day! One morning while I was on the scale, I heard a gentle whisper from God, "Do not desire to see what I do not want you to see, but only desire to see what I want you to see." I understood this whisper and I realized that God was asking me to trust Him instead.

A few days later another one of His gentle whispers came to me, "Give me one day a week, and then you can enjoy eating meals for the rest of the week." It was clear to me that my God was asking me to devote a day of the week to prayer and fasting. But the intention was not to be about me, but about Him. He let me know that I should not only abstain from food, but also from obsessively weighing myself. I began to give up food one day a week and, on that day, to pray more intently.

I chose Tuesday because I enjoyed going to church on that day to receive Holy Communion (This is the Bread of Life to me). Fasting on this day would make it even more meaningful and joyful. I began fasting every Tuesday from my waking until dinner time, relying on only liquids for my physical sustenance. When my stomach started to growl for food or when I felt faint, I would go to prayer. I would speak Scripture to my stomach, "Man does not live on bread alone...so stop growling!" In the beginning I struggled, but as I allowed myself to be trained in this discipline, my stomach's complaints ceased. As it became easier, I realized I was more joyful, alert, and energetic! My stomach began to obey me instead of the other way around.

I was realizing the benefits of fasting and prayer! I had finally lost the weight and my foot pain was gone, but that was not my focus or my purpose in fasting. My intention was the enjoyment of an intimate time with God which was made possible through a clear mind. Every time I felt hungry or in need of energy, I trusted my God to take care of my needs as I entered into prayer.

Fasting and prayer was about being obedient to whispers I heard from Him. I wanted to find and obey God's will and His direction for my life. I wanted to seek Him without expecting any gain for myself. My relationship with God was my focus. I needed to give up my self-oriented goals.

Ultimately, I received much more than just physical healings. Yes, my foot pain was finally gone, and my weight went down and even another persistent physical issue that I had dealt with since childhood resolved itself. I was healed of all these bodily things. But also, I came to know my God better as He was addressing all my needs, inside and out, and even the ones I hadn't brought directly to Him! This knowledge of His love, and of His care for me and for my personal needs created a vibrant and more youthful spirit within me. Often, and without thought, I found myself experiencing the abandoned joy that children so freely express.

Then came the Coronavirus pandemic. I saw race rioting on the news with all the violence and looting. I felt the pain, suffering and evilness and, also my helplessness to make a difference. So, I turned to the only thing I know to do; fasting and prayer to seek His healing grace for unity and righteousness for everyone on earth. In doing this, I was prompted by God to fast for the entire month of June. I would include our country and our civil strife in my prayers. I shared this with Fran, and she decided to join me for the month of June. It was intense. We fasted every day during the week, except for weekends. Monday through Friday we would sustain ourselves only on liquids until breaking our fast for dinner.

Fasting for my purposes or for my gain proved unsuccessful and even unbearable; I could not sustain it. It exhausted and discouraged me. It became obvious that my previous understanding and approach to fasting was not biblical. It was not a truly spiritual fast. I learned that

God's goal for my fasting was not about any results that might come, but in fact, the fasting was more about God than about me! I started to see that God's goal for me to endure physical emptiness was to, in turn, discover a fuller connection with Him. The results, any results, would then be of His will and His doing and for His glory and I would be the obedient servant seeking His outcomes.

How can God be glorified by our fasting? When we deny our comfort and dependence on food, and pray for His heart and His will, seeking His face for any situation, without expecting any results in return, then He alone is glorified. This kind of fasting is holy and pleasing to Him. Our strength to endure this kind of fasting comes from God and not from our willpower. Relying on our strength alone, and wanting our needs to be met, robs us of the joy of giving up. It becomes merely a discipline, not a holy pursuit. But as we seek Him first and endure slight suffering for His glory, our hardship becomes a Holy offering, born out of our love for Him. Through surrendering and obeying, we learn to trust in Him more and more and thereby grow our faith as we train ourselves to deny ourselves and practice this wonderful spiritual exercise!

After enjoying this king of holy fasting and encouraging others to do the same, one day God wrote below in my heart.

1. Fasting is a time to feast in prayer, meditation, and scripture.

2. Denying worldly dependence creates an atmosphere for the Holy Spirit to talk to us. Scriptures become alive and our mind is more attentive to hear and process His whispers.

3. When I enter into prayer on an empty stomach or by denying oneself our habitual distractions (those who are not able to go without food for medical reasons could deny what you crave. It could be social media, phone, TV, computer, etc...), I am humbled to deny my control over things of this world, especially from taking comfort in food, and instead, depend on divine providence.

4. Satan hates this kind of fasting because it trains us to build up our characters like Jesus. In Luke 4:4 Jesus said when he was tempted by Satan, *Man does not live on bread alone, but on every word that comes from the mouth of God.*

5. This kind of fasting; fasting for the glory of God (seeking the Will and Heart of God) without seeking any rewards, is holy and most pleasing to God. It can become a joyful process for our souls when we seek only spiritual food to sustain us, rather than relying on physical nourishment to fill our needs and desires.

The most important lesson I have learned is that when we live a life for the glory of God, we do not even have to ask God as He sees the needs and desires of our heart, and even before we ask, He will give it to us. Psalm 37:4 teaches us that when we take delight in the Lord, He will give us the desires of our heart. This means that we have learned and trained ourselves to align our desires with His desires. Praying for His Heart and His Will become joyful for us and of an utmost importance, superseding even our own perceived needs. When we develop this confidence and love to go before God to enjoy His presence, without a 'to do' list when praying, it is holy and pleasing to our God. In this confidence, it is also joyful to pray, "May your will be done, not mine," and then we will be content and happy in every situation. This attitude of heart will eliminate the desires to have what others have and what we perceive we don't have. When we live a life for His glory, the fullest contentment and joy becomes ours as we become fully united with Him!

Have you ever thought of fasting without expecting anything back in return? Or for a change, how about fasting from social media or TV or cell phone? See if it will make a difference in the attitude of your heart.

SOME FINAL THOUGHTS

Are You Thirsty and Hungry for God? (Pam & Fran)
In John 7:37b, Jesus said, *"Let anyone who is thirsty come to me and drink."* Do you understand that He desires to be more present to us than we could ever realize? It is the Creator's desire to communicate Himself to His created, and we only need to seek God in daily and simple moments and entertain His presence, for it to become as easy and natural as breathing.

Will you not be thirsty and hungry after an afternoon of exercising or walking in the hot sun? It's easy enough then to be replenished with a refreshing drink and something to eat. Our spiritual life is much the same! We must nurture it and care for it as we do our bodies. When we consciously make it a point to entertain His presence in every given moment, we will no longer find ourselves thirsting and needing more of God. When we do this, it will be a refreshment to our souls, like a cool drink on a hot sunny day. When we abide in Him, He abides in us.

If we leave God in the churches, we will soon become dry and thirsty. But when we enjoy His living presence through simple daily moments, we will never go thirsty and we find that we will be filled with excitement and joy. When we are able to be still and enjoy His presence, we will also hear His whispers all the time. It could be as simple as Fran looking into the blue sky and hearing holy whispers or enjoying the Creator through His creation of a leaf. In these moments there is only God and Fran in the world and His presence becomes so real that it is as though she can really touch Him. His presence is a gracious gift to us so we can grow and enjoy His world abundantly.

While Moses was tending the flock, he saw a burning bush and he decided to go and see it. Exodus 3:3, "So Moses thought, 'I will go over and see this strange sight—why the bush does not burn up.'" Strange, yet he did not ignore it, but obeyed the whisper of a strange sight. Had he not obeyed the calling to go up, how would he hear the voice of God? If he did not obey, how could he perform all the miracles? It all starts with a simple whisper followed by our obedience and then miracles happen. Have you had strange thoughts to help someone? Or a strong compulsion to do something for someone's gain? Or a strange thought that provokes greater thoughts? Don't procrastinate, it could be God's gentle whispers trying to start a conversation with you!

Jesus says in John 8:47, "He who belongs to God hears what God says. The reason you do not hear is that you do not belong to God." Pharisees had the book knowledge, but they missed recognizing the Messiah. If our knowledge is limited to the books in the Bible, we can miss hearing when God whispers. Don't let your biblical knowledge rob you of the precious moments to connect to the living God.

There are three voices that can run through our minds: our own voice, God's voice, or Satan's voice. How can we know the difference? Be still, go to God in prayer and have patience until God provides a confirmation (opening the door or closing the door), so we do not twist these voices for our gain to do what we want to do. When we train ourselves in confirming and overcoming the hurdles that ensue with these whispers, we get to experience firsthand how God gives us the strength to *"press on toward the goal to win the prize for which God has called me heavenward in Christ Jesus."* (Phil 3:14) A good example of listening and obeying God's whispers to a good outcome, is in reading this book that we have written to share with you!

Prayer is the best way to get in touch with the truth and reality of God Himself. If we are ever doubtful of whose whispers we are hearing, we must go to God in prayer, and also turn to Scripture. God can handle all our doubts and questions. He will train our mind and give it the right direction so that we can discern His voice over ours and other voices. It is the most basic and supernatural experience when we go before Him, sitting still without a to-do list. The Holy Spirit will allow us to pray through Him. Prayer changes the attitude of the heart to see things differently; the way God wants us to see through His eyes. Supernatural ability could be achieved only by going to God in prayer and living in scripture, as it says in 2 Timothy 3:16-17, where it tells us, *"All Scripture is God-breathed and is useful for teaching, rebuking, correcting, and training in righteousness, so that the servant of God may be thoroughly equipped for every good work."* Surely, He will clarify our thoughts and teach us the right direction. So that we will be trained by Him to discern His holy whispers.

Prayer is not a matter of expecting miracles or that of taking a 'to do list', but a road to build an intimate relationship with the mighty God of this universe through whispering, communicating back and forth. It ignites a spark of energy to make life exciting and hopeful in all circumstances. Prayer has the power to change the world. Prayer also can work miracles in a person's inner nature which can transform us. By bringing our daily tasks to God, good and bad, He can show us the fuller meaning of them and invite us into the greater depth of His love for His people. Our wills, God's, and ours, then become one!!!

Please visit us at
TheGodWhoWhispers.com
and share your own stories.

PAM FERNANDO is a woman comfortable in many cultures. She was born in Sri Lanka, where she grew up and then married Clive. They left Sri Lanka and eventually ended up in the United States in 1989, making their forever home in Texas, where they have raised their two sons.

Pam enjoyed being a homemaker during most of her boys' lives until she entered the corporate world when her youngest began high school. She became the Chief Financial Officer for a local company. However, upon meeting and holding her first grandchild, Bethel, Pam was convicted to leave the corporate world and begin her own consulting business. Meanwhile, she also enjoyed serving God through short term mission work in Guatemala, Honduras, Peru, India, and Uganda.

Eventually, Pam felt God calling her to fully devote herself to helping people locally and throughout the world. She found a special calling in the work of healing and prayer through the Order of Saint Luke (OSL), healing ministry for years and has established a healing center in Pittsburgh, Pennsylvania. Her greatest joy and gift are in helping those in need, and all for the glory of God.

Pam and Clive and their youngest son reside in Plano, Texas, while their oldest and his family, and their grandchildren live in Pittsburgh, Pennsylvania.

FRAN ROSEBERRY was born into a family of artists, grew up on Long Island, and graduated with a degree in Art Education from Skidmore College in Saratoga Springs, NY.

Fran and her husband David met while he was a seminarian and she was the Secretary to the Vice President of Church Divinity School of the Pacific in Berkeley, CA. The year after David's graduation, while serving at a church in Tucson, AZ, they were married.

After moving their growing family to Texas and for the following 31 years, David and Fran planted and ministered together at Christ Church in Plano. In the early years Fran helped start and support many of the ministries and served on the church staff a number of times. Later her love for hospitality and her heart for the clergy spouses and prayer became her focus. Throughout those years Fran freelanced as a calligrapher. In the 1990's David and Fran began a travel ministry and together have led over thirty pilgrimages to Israel and other locations around the world where the Christian heritage can be experienced. This ministry is still ongoing and she loves it.

They have four grown children, two of whom are married, an adopted son in Canada, and five grandchildren. Fran and David attend Restoration Anglican Church in Richardson. She attends a neighborhood Bible Study, loves to paint, and cherishes time with family and friends.

Pam Fernando and Fran Roseberry have done a wonderful service in writing, "The God Who Whispers." It provides a spirituality which is focused in the here and now and enables the reader to grasp how God guides us in the most ordinary situations. This book makes living in the presence of God, a matter of listening and responding to the everyday whispering of the God who loves us and is intimately attending to every moment of our lives.

—REV. JOSEPH ACTON
Founder & Executive Director
of Desert Call Ministries,
Author, Teacher, & North American Director
of the Order of St. Luke the Physician (OSL)

One could buy several books in hopes of learning what Fran & Pam reveal to us through their stories. In sharing their experiences they have unwittingly made the complex simple! We soon discover how deeply personal our God is and how much He wants to be in relationship with us! Their book delights and challenges us and they pray that as we're reading, we will come to recognize the God who whispers in our own lives. Enjoy the journey and prepare to be transformed!

—KAREN BEDFORD
Wife, mother, grandmother,
friend, career volunteer
and servant of God

If you ever wonder whether God has time for you, The God Who Whispers, will satisfy your soul's longing, and light your path. The authors share their incredible, personal, and prayerful experiences which result from intentionally listening to the heart of God and obeying His direction.

You will close this book filled up and over with joy in knowing that God is an ever-loving, and ever-faithful Presence. When you take a moment to breathe Him in, you will hear His whispers loud and clear. He speaks to you all the time, and He doesn't want you to miss anything He has already planned for you. Go, and live in His joy!

—KAREN MOORE
AUTHOR OF IT'S STILL POSSIBLE
AND OVER 100 INSPIRATIONAL BOOKS

At some point in our lives many of us have asked these pivotal questions: Why am I here? What is my purpose? Is there a God? Does he know about and care for me personally? How can I hear His voice? What is His will for me?

This collection of awesome testimonies by the two amazing ladies who seek to hear God and follow Him will encourage all of us as we journey through life's uncertainties and try to navigate the uncharted waters to our true home.

I recommend this book to all who are trying to find wholeness in the midst of our chaotic times.

—DR MIKE SABBACK
PHYSICIAN, SURGEON AND OSL CONVENER

Like King David, who was a man after God's own heart, Pam and Fran are two saints in Christ who seek the heart of God. And, in seeking God's heart they find His love, His goodness and His presence in miraculous ways. It is my prayer that this book, which is full of encounters with Christ, will fill your soul and spark a passion within your heart to thirst after The Lord's presence yourself because "in His presence is the fullness of joy!

—TROG TROGDON
AUTHOR OF "A WALK TO WISDOM"
& URBAN MISSIONARY

Soli
Deo
Gloria

From Beginning to End